THE CURIOUS CASE
of the
BOARDING SCHOOL

Mahnaz Mir, 14, has been writing ever since she learnt how to, beginning from small notes to her parents to letters, essays, articles and short stories, most of which have been published in newspapers and magazines for readers of her age. She has also won several interschool prizes for art and creative writing in English, and recently a bronze medal in the International Kangaroo Linguistic Contest 2019. Having visited the US, England, Canada, Turkey, Thailand, Scotland, Malaysia and the UAE with her family, she plans on using these experiences as inspirations for her forthcoming work.

Mahnaz has been blogging at www.mahnazmir.blogspot.com since she was eight. *The Curious Case of the Boarding School* is her debut novel.

THE CURIOUS CASE *of the* BOARDING SCHOOL

Mahnaz Mir

RUPA

Published by
Rupa Publications India Pvt. Ltd 2020
7/16, Ansari Road, Daryaganj
New Delhi 110002

Sales centres:
Allahabad Bengaluru Chennai
Hyderabad Jaipur Kathmandu
Kolkata Mumbai

Copyright © Mahnaz Mir 2020

All rights reserved.

No part of this publication may be reproduced, transmitted, or stored in a retrieval system, in any form or by any means, electronic, mechanical, photocopying, recording or otherwise, without the prior permission of the publisher.

This is a work of fiction. Names, characters, places and incidents are either the product of the author's imagination or are used fictitiously and any resemblance to any actual person, living or dead, events or locales is entirely coincidental.

978-93-90356-47-8

First impression 2020

10 9 8 7 6 5 4 3 2 1

The moral right of the author has been asserted.

Printer at HT Media Ltd, Gr. Noida

This book is sold subject to the condition that it shall not, by way of trade or otherwise, be lent, resold, hired out, or otherwise circulated, without the publisher's prior consent, in any form of binding or cover other than that in which it is published.

For my mother

ONE

The bell rang shrilly at the end of the seventh period. The boys, already waiting for the boring Geography lesson to end, had shoved their books into their bags without even waiting for the teacher to finish.

'Bell, teacher, bell!' they all chanted in a well-practised chorus. The teacher, who was left with no choice, gave up, walked from the centre of the classroom to the front and stood behind the rostrum, packing up her own transparent slides, lecture notes, homework notebooks and whatnots. At the same time, the boys excitedly rushed out of their class. Some of them yelled 'bye-bye, teacher' and received a smile and nod in return, while the others just yelled at one another, making use of the few minutes of freedom they had with their friends before their parents came to take them home.

Sameer had been living for a month as a boarder at the school, and today, unlike the rest of his day-scholar classmates, he had no plans. He had not been chummy with anyone in particular. Being a small-town boy left alone in the big metropolitan city to study, fend for himself and socialize on his own, things were not as easy for him as his parents had promised they would be. He silently packed his bag, fastened every section of his satchel carefully, took out his multisectioned pencil case and put back every item of stationery where it belonged. He had no idea that his teacher was observing him closely but she had decided to be a silent spectator for a couple of weeks before helping him out to make friends with the rest of the boys. She had had a newcomer every year and knew the drill: The new boy would always find it hard to pierce through the strong bonds of friendship the older students had formed through the years, but would eventually mingle.

She saw him finally lift his head. Sameer was startled to see the teacher looking at him. She simply waved a farewell to which he shyly smiled, lowered his head and walked out of the room. The teacher sighed, for she knew that in some time, the rowdiness of the other boisterous kids would rub off on him and he too, would become someone far from shy, quiet and meek.

Sameer turned back once again, just to see that the teacher, now burnt out because of constant lecturing, had put her head on the table. Once he was out in the corridor, he looked around to see the boys, some were his classmates, some strangers, and both older and younger students. Boys in all shapes, sizes and colours—stout, thin, tall, short, dark, ivory, super stylish, plain;

Kingston High had an extremely colourful milieu. He saw some boys chatting in pairs, and some showing off the newest gadget their parents had got for them. He even recognized a few from his class. They were nice kids and probably could be good for company, but his encouraging brain always failed him against his discouraging feet.

He stood still in the corridor like a surveyor, and his attention shifted from the population of the school to the building. He found himself mesmerized by the huge red structure. It is said that when buildings become as old as time, they develop a life of their own. Sameer had read a few stories that had enchanted edifices and he found his school's building glaring at him every time he had to go to the canteen or even visit the grounds. The security officers standing here and there and especially, at the heights, would intimidate Sameer.

Walking to the nearest canteen, he inwardly laughed at the fact that despite having a dozen canteens throughout the school, every one of them was overcrowded. The boys, each one hungrier or thirstier than the other, were pushing and shoving, while demanding water, soft drinks and the ever-popular samosas. His stomach rumbled like that of a hungry lion on a prowl. Sameer grabbed his belly to try and hush it, fearing that someone would hear it. He still looked around, alarmed, for he didn't handle embarrassment too well. His brain told him to chill, for the noise in the canteen was too much for anyone to hear the growls inside his stomach.

The hostel's mess was about a kilometer away. It was almost time for the school shuttle to pick up the kids and transport them to the boarding houses, both being within walled premises. However, today Sameer decided to walk. He took off his heavy backpack and decided to tug it along his side, like an attaché case. As he came closer to the mess, he could smell something being fried. He was anticipating a good wholesome plateful of pulao, just like the one his mother made for him. He pictured the aroma wafting out of a huge frying pan in which the portly school chef was frying numerous aloo tikkis to accompany the heavenly pulao.

But he was in for a slight disappointment when lunch was served, for it was a day of burgers and fries. He had realized within one month of living apart from his family that he could live with the once-a-week-allowance of junk food by his health-conscious mother, but he couldn't help missing his mom's home-cooked meals. Strangely, he even missed his sisters' utterly annoying habit of poking fun at him at the dinner table. The boys were harsher in their pranks. Food fights, spilling water down each other's collars, wiping dirty hands on another's trousers and so on. He had learnt that sitting alone was better for him, especially when laundry day was far off.

The rest of the day went by writing an assignment

that was due the following week, and sleeping, of course. However, he couldn't sleep easily as the stress of the upcoming football game he had would torture him for the next few days until it would finally pass. Sometimes, Sameer even regretted opting for the trials and getting selected for the team. He had intentionally missed the practice session that day, and while that should have helped him relax and feel refreshed, it greatly worsened the anxiety. He made a mental promise to himself to participate in at least two of the five field practices held every day, and decided to skip the daily horse riding lessons until the game. The teacher could be told he had sprained his foot. Thankfully, the riding field and the football ground were at different ends of the school.

Being a teenager, keeping himself entertained was not very hard. He would read his monthly sci-fi magazine that his mother had promised to send regularly through post. She sent his basic necessities, too, such as cereal, new clothes, a tin of his favourite chocolates that he had to eat sensibly until the next batch arrived thirty days later, and a foil tray full of home-made hazelnut-filled chocolates, which he shared with his classmates and teachers. Sameer plugged in his earphones and switched on a playlist that relaxed him the most, and gradually dozed off.

The following day, everything seemed to be messed up. Sameer had woken up really late and almost missed breakfast. He also forgot to tuck in his shirt, which made the headmaster glare at him during assembly. And now, he just couldn't concentrate on his game.

Whenever Sameer tried to shut his mind off of everything else and focus on the game, he would panic even more. Despite being told that the team was 'more prepared than needed' and that he should stop overthinking, Sameer convinced his team to play one more game. He heard Fahad and Mustapha whine about still having to decorate the school auditorium for an upcoming event, but Sameer managed to convince them that the game, though already perfected, would stay in their bones if practised just one more time.

After the practice, which went well, the boys, all sweaty, tired and drained, left for their homes or the hostel. Sameer headed for a shower, for if there was one thing that irked him, it was stench—and his clothes and hair both reeked of sweat, dust and grime. In the shower, he replayed in his mind the errors they were making and his discussions with the other players. He also recalled how easy it was for him to be a 'bro' with the boys on the field, and decided to try being as easygoing off the field as he was on it.

Once back in the room, Sameer looked at his checklist. A lot was left to be done. His plans included downloading new music to his iPod shuffle, decorating the hostel corridors with his fellow boarders and a good amount of exercising at the gym.

Somehow he felt stressed and confused for a reason yet unknown to himself. Maybe he missed home and his two dogs. Or was it something about the school's eeriness that bothered him? Trying his best to ignore it, he decided to play the guitar to soothe his nerves. It actually did help a lot, and was better than any kind of yoga or meditation he had tried. He went to the rooftop so that no one would hear him and make fun of him later, and played for half an hour.

Just before bedtime, his mom Skyped him for almost an hour, something that also brought him a measure of ease. His mother's encouraging words made him determined and he was grateful that despite her busy schedule, she always made time to talk to him once or twice a week. He felt positive about his game and his mom's pep talk helped further. Life was getting easier, he thought, as he drifted off to sleep.

⁓

The sun had risen. It was a Sunday. He visited the school gym first thing in the morning. He then went on to warm up for the day's practice, after which he partnered up with a teammate, who just so happened to be an early riser, too. He, however, couldn't participate in a final practice with the entire team since most of the players were still asleep in their dorms. Sunday was usually a lazy day for the boarders since there was little homework to catch up on. For Sameer, a rare productive Sunday consisted of practice in the morning, a nap at noon and some light studying in the evening. That Sunday, however, the boys had decided to plan on how to decorate the dorms, auditorium and hallways for the themed farewell party for the graduates. The party was three weeks later, but the boys wanted it to be the coolest party ever, and thought of various tricks and displays that they could put up. The theme of the party that had been agreed upon after several debates was: 'SPOOKY'.

⌒

After a hard day's work, Sameer was satisfied and ready for a great game the following morning. He replayed his mother's advice in his head, until waves of sleep washed over him, making him fall fast asleep.

On the day of the game, Sameer woke up early. He felt determined to win his first-ever inter-school game. He was also nervous, as he was competing with one of the best football teams in the state.

He courageously walked towards the grounds. The field was empty except for the maintainers and cleaners doing the last of their chores and the gym teacher and sports coach supervising them. Sameer greeted his teacher and coach, got a pat of approval from the latter for being punctual and was told to take five rounds of the ground to warm up. Sameer looked at Coach Malik in silent protest, but Coach Malik put a hand on his shoulder and said, 'You will be replacing Rauf as the co-captain. That kid is good, but you have shown more promise and dedication. In my team, hard work never goes to waste. Just keep this news to yourself and I shall announce it later, after the game ends.' Sameer was overwhelmed.

'Right now, I want you to play and lead the team like a co-captain would. I shall ask Rauf to step back a little,' Coach Malik continued as Sameer's spirit touched the sky. He felt warmed up already, proud and happy that his hard work had paid off.

Soon, the opponent team arrived. Sameer sized every boy up as they stretched and spot-jogged on the field. He also did a headcount of his team members as they started dropping in one by one.

At last, with the signal of a high-pitched whistle, the game began. The ball, placed in the centre of the field, was first kicked by the opposing team. Sameer was extremely frustrated when his own school's boys rooted for the other team because they had been winning the house game consecutively for the past five years. As soon as they were into the game, Sameer could see their secret to success: they played in unison. This year, Coach Malik had taught them to play as one, but Sameer was doubtful whether the boys had it in them to beat the strong team that had already put them under pressure.

TWO

When the whistle was blown to indicate that half of the game was over, neither team had scored a goal. The game was tough. The guest team was playing offensive and the home team was on the defensive. The goalie was given continuous shout-outs by Coach Malik and the boys. He had been giving his best and the other team was a bit surprised, for they had come with instant victory in mind. The second half saw the teams reverse their roles. The house team's goalie was still on his toes, attentive to the minutest of details and the house players were trying to score by hook or by crook. Several times — six to be exact — the ball bounced off the goal's iron frame and the goalie of the opponent team seemed a little unnerved.

In the last few minutes, Rauf, the co-captain, had the ball. He tackled it well, defending it from the other team, but when he was surrounded by them all just near the goal, he kicked it backwards to captain Faizan, who was on the right side of the goal. Faizan tackled the ball and slipped it cautiously to Rizwan, who was standing next to him. Rizwan tossed it between his feet, but soon couldn't tackle it anymore. Just then, Sameer ran up to help out. Once he had control of the ball, he shouted, 'To the striker!'

The opposing team turned their attention to Rauf, the one closest to the goal and the striker. Sameer sensed an opportunity, so he dodged the ball away from everyone and kicked it straight into the goal from the left.

Everything came to a standstill until Saqib, the goalie from Sameer's team, yelled from his post, 'GOOOOAAAAAL!'

Celebrations, shout-outs, pats and tarzan calls broke out around the field. The players went crazy and so did the spectators. Sameer was a hero! Praised and congratulated, he received much love from everyone.

As soon as he got back to his dorm room, the first person Sameer called was his mother. He also begged her to not share the news with all the eight billion people on earth through her Facebook and Instagram accounts. 'But it's a proud moment, Beta,' she was ecstatic.

'Yeah, but just keep it to yourself!' he almost hissed.

'Nah,' his mother was too happy to listen to him. 'Not happening. I am already thinking of hashtags! "SameerSuperhero"! How does that sound?'

Sameer facepalmed, but didn't say anything because he knew his mom couldn't help bragging. So, he bade her goodbye and received tons of flying kisses in return.

'Whew!' he said to himself. He was happy. Very

happy! But he was also a little nervous about how Rauf would react to the coach's decision. But that could wait, he thought. He really deserved a timeout from all this uncertainty.

Just as he was about to rest, a boy called Saleem came panting down the hallway as if he had been running for miles.

'Sameer! Sameer! Sameer!'

Sameer poked his head out of the door, surprised and a little freaked out.

'What?' he asked.

'Co...Coach...' Saleem was out of breath. 'Coach Malik wants us all in the changing room,' he finally managed to say.

Yikes, Sameer thought. It was time for *the* talk.

'Okay, I'm coming,' Sameer said calmly.

Saleem put his hands up, 'I am done, dude. You go around the east wing of the hostel and tell Babar and Azeem, and around the North Wing to tell Khurram and Rizwan.'

'Okay...' Sameer said after a short pause, not quite amused by being ordered around.

'Yep,' Saleem said a little more bossily.

Sameer put his trainers on, and went off to perform the errands. When he reached the changing room, the scene before his eyes was not what he had expected. He had imagined a very serious talk taking place between the players and the coach, but it was actually a party!

Coach Malik had rewarded the team with an impromptu party. There was food from the coolest brands of burgers, pasta, pizzas and pies, and loads and loads of cold drinks, which were otherwise banned on the school campus. There were also paper cups filled with black, orange, light green and transparent sodas, lined up to be downed by the Player of the Game. The boys were chattering loudly, and goofing around. A group of four or five boys was even replaying their moves from the game in a corner. Coach Malik, a huge, muscly, bald guy, who was well respected by the players, came to the front of the room and asked for attention in his loud, growly voice. His face had a wide grin instead of the usual scowl.

'Congratulations, boys! Well played! We showed 'em!'

There was wild clapping and cheering, followed by wolf whistles. 'All of you played very well. I am very proud of you, and so is the entire school. We have the award ceremony tomorrow during the school assembly where you shall all be given the certificates and trophies that you very well deserve. I am also going to announce the Player of the Game.'

There was pin-drop silence in the room. Everyone was waiting for this moment. Some of them had even bet it would be the team captain Faizan, but others had the new boy in mind.

'So, I am going to pull you guys out of your misery,

and make *the* announcement. It is Sameer Abbas!'

There was silence in the crowded room. It was a huge surprise. 'The new boy?' someone said from the back of the room. The coach looked questioningly towards the crowd, but no one said anything else.

'Yes,' said the coach finally, feeling the discomfort in the room. 'We are very happy to have such a talented addition to the team. Clap for him, boys. Don't be so mean,' the coach added and the boys clapped. Rizwan and Azeem patted Sameer on the back, whose face was flushed as he was too embarrassed and happy at the same time. But he had seen the look on the face of the one person who had not been happy at the announcement—Faizan, the team captain. Sameer sensed tension in his voice even when he congratulated him.

This is not a good start, Sameer thought.

'Drink it! Drink it! Drink it!' the boys started chanting and Sameer was pushed to the table where he had to gulp down the soda in twenty paper cups. He managed to drink seven, with hardly enough breaks to breathe and then let out such a huge and noisy burp that the boys went crazy with laughter. The drinking game soon turned into a belching game, where the boys drank by the bottle, and competed to let out the loudest burp.

In between the fun and laughter, someone slipped a note into Sameer's fist. When he looked up, he couldn't make out who might have done it. He unfurled the note. It said, 'Meet me in the activity room.' Sameer was confused, but decided to go anyway.

Once there, he looked about but saw no one. Not very amused by pranks, Sameer was about to leave the place and head back to his dorm room when he heard a voice, 'Hello! Someone here?'

Sameer was startled.

'Hello, who and where are you?' Sameer asked in return in a very formal manner, guessing it was one of his football teammates, trying to play a prank on him. He was proven to be right when, upon turning around, he recognized Ravi from the team. Ravi began introducing himself—he wanted to give the new co-captain a good first impression.

'Y' know, I'm on the team, mate,' Ravi said. 'Oh, and congratulations on your first victory!'

'Thanks!'

Feeling around for the switchboard, Sameer turned on a few lights. He paused for a second before asking, 'You're here for the—' only to be interrupted by the annoying boy again.

'Ceremony, yes.'

Turning his attention back to the room, Sameer saw tables and chairs, a Superman cake, which Sameer was embarrassed by (the team consisted of teenagers, not kids!), three ghost figures, since it was the most conveniently available item of decoration as the boys had been preparing for the spooky party, and, of course, party poppers. The boys on the football team had not had enough of the official party and so, they had already planned one of their own.

Sameer was interrupted from his daze when a group of loud, chattering students burst in through the door. It seemed that the players had invited their friends over, too. Word had spread fast, Sameer realized, as everyone paused to look at him. Maybe there was a downside to being made co-captain so unexpectedly, after all.

Sameer felt awkward being the centre of attention, but figured he would have to get used to it. All the boys stared at Sameer as if he had done something horrific. He panicked. The coach wasn't around anymore, and Sameer could only think the worst. He thought the boys would make fun of him and bully him. He wasn't *really* excited about having replaced Rauf as the co-captain — the team was fond of Rauf, and he wondered whether they would accept him as the new co-captain. Sameer hadn't realized he was shaking until he felt a tap on the shoulder. It was Ravi.

'You okay, mate?' he said, 'You look like you've seen a ghost.'

'Perfectly fine,' Sameer answered, not wanting to draw attention to himself.

'Okay,' someone else said, not convinced at all, 'Just chill out, yeah?'

Sameer nodded.

Not long after, he heard the loud, booming sound of

a party popper, thinking that it definitely deafened him.

A chorus of cheers was heard while simultaneously another party popper was burst. Sameer put his hands over his ears to protect them from the loud booms. He was annoyed.

The boys, including Sameer, then walked over to the teacher's desk where they cut the cake, and the Player of the Game was fed the 'hand' of Superman by Ravi.

Sameer was dragged into playing a game of Truth or Dare, and was taunted for not choosing a dare five times in a row. Finally, he challenged the boys to give him a difficult dare. Half a minute later, he struggled to position Ravi on his back, as he had dared to give him a piggyback ride. It was not exactly easy, considering he was twice Sameer's size.

'If I fall, I'll kill you!' Ravi yelled.

'Don't worry, I do strength training every day,' Sameer responded sassily.

As he was almost about to give up, Sameer surprised himself when he started to effortlessly run around the room, despite Ravi's weight. His successful completion of the dare was accompanied by cheers and whistles, astounded faces and a yelling Ravi.

After a few more seconds, Sameer dropped Ravi onto the teacher's desk with a loud thud. Ravi sprang up and furiously ran towards Sameer, who raced for the door. The sight was hilarious, and the other boys started laughing.

It was midnight and the boys were wondering whether to continue with their game, when they saw that Rizwan had slumped against the wall and dozed off. So, they decided to call it a night.

Ravi, on the other hand, chased Sameer till he lost him in the area of the dorm rooms. Clearly, he didn't have the time or patience to knock on every door to search for his target.

After almost an hour of waiting for Ravi to come barging in, Sameer lay down in bed to have a good night's sleep. Thinking of the party made him chuckle. In spite of it being extremely silly and immature, it was satisfying. Even his childhood dream had come true that day — being captain of the football team! Well, co-captain, he reminded himself.

He set his alarm for the next day, excited and happy. He had finally made friends. More than anything, the feeling of being an outsider in the school had faded today, providing hope for better days.

Before he knew it, Sameer was sound asleep.

THREE

The sun shone bright on Sameer's face. The chirps and trills of different birds could be heard in the otherwise dead-silent dorm room. He woke up with a groan, only to realize that it was still pretty early. To put his awakened senses back to sleep, he lay on his stomach with his head underneath his feathery soft pillow. His final thought before dozing off once more was, 'Why is the sun so bright at forty-five past five in the morning?'

Sameer had been dreaming of the library back home, which he missed oh so much, only to be interrupted by his obnoxiously loud alarm clock.

'Uggghh!'

Barely a second before he punched the alarm clock, a familiar face appeared in the doorway. In his still groggy state, Sameer questioned the boy.

'What are you doing here?' he asked, already aware of the answer. Ravi had obviously come looking for revenge, or so Sameer thought.

'Not up yet, I see,' said Ravi. He hadn't entered Sameer's room, nor attacked him. Ravi was a bit surprised at the fact that no one was up and about like him yet.

Sameer's alarm indicated that it was six and he was sitting up in an alert state for two reasons. It was time to get up anyway, but also to get ready for another episode of 'Run from Ravi.' Sameer thought for a split second, and then said, 'I'm sorry, please stop chasing me. Let's call it a truce.' Sameer stretched out a hand.

'I'm kidding, bro. Chill out.'

'So, what *are* you doing at this time anyway?' Sameer asked.

'I've been up for a gazillion hours, so basically, B-O-R-E-D.' Ravi spelt out the word for emphasis. 'Don't even know how I ended up with y'all weird dudes.'

'First of all, I am not weird,' Sameer retorted. 'No, wait. *You* are the weird one.'

Sameer lazily got out of his bed. His legs froze instantly, as he put his feet on the cold floor. 'And secondly, we need to get to the campus. We've unnecessarily wasted quite a lot of time and it is...' Sameer paused to look at his watch, 'fifteen past six.'

He said this very nonchalantly, but as soon as the reality dawned on him, Sameer's eyes popped open, without even needing to splash water on his face. 'Oh my god! My first class is at seven!'

'I would appreciate you going back to your dorm,' Sameer said to Ravi. He was trying to be warm, while at the same time, shoving Ravi out of the doorway with a quick 'bye'.

Sameer's heart went out to Ravi, as he too was away

from his home. He had himself arrived in the big city and had been feeling intimidated by his surroundings. One could only imagine how uncomfortable it could feel to jump an entire country just to attend school. He must be very adaptable, this Ravi guy, Sameer thought, impressed by his easy-going personality.

Sameer got dressed frantically, skipped the boring breakfast of aloo paratha in the mess and reached his first class just on time. The past few weeks had been hectic. While he would normally have enough time before his classes to doodle, these days he could barely breathe.

The first semester's most happening football game was over, but somehow, Sameer felt a light pressure all the time, though he was unable to figure out why. Maybe it was the weird vibe he got from Faizan and Rauf, mostly while at practice. Or it could have been academic stress, due to his poor time management. Sameer also had to stay away from his guitar. His reputation was just building up and he certainly didn't want to be known as a 'guitar-playing softie'.

Although the previous night had been an icebreaker with some of the kids at school and he had received and returned more 'hi' and 'hola' than ever before, the building of the school still had that eerie effect on him. Maybe the school was haunted. Sameer tried his best to ignore the spooky feeling and focused on what was important. It would probably take more than a few weeks for him to completely settle down. *At least,* the teachers had quit staring at him with what he thought were murderous glares from time to time.

But Sameer was soon going to find himself being a target of another group of boys—the infamous school bullies. Sameer had never thought that bullying would be a problem at Kingston High.

But it was.

Sameer wasn't specifically attacked yet, but most other boys had been targeted by this group. Thinking they were extremely cool, this band of five ran around the school, particularly at lunch break, giving random and embarrassing nicknames to whoever they felt like. They had no purpose in life, except to annoy people.

These older boys would also shove, poke and boss over younger students, while making fun of them openly. Sameer pitied the innocent boys who would laugh along, completely unaware that they were being ridiculed. Moreover, these apparently 'cool' guys ordered their 'servants'—the eighth-grade students—to get them stuff from the canteens. Since they were graduating and were in the limelight, their 'celebrity status' had gone to their heads.

Despite not liking what he saw, Sameer couldn't speak up. Each time he would be on the verge of spitting something out, but he held himself back, always regretting it later.

However, Sameer had sworn to butt in if they made

a scene that day. He was determined to feel strong and positive, even if things didn't go as planned. After the first period had passed, Sameer eagerly waited for lunch break. Skipping breakfast, after all, had not been the greatest idea.

The school bell finally rang. Without hesitating, Sameer was the first one to rush out of class. He finally stopped running and panicking, thinking it would be best to figure out the situation, on the spot.

Sameer was aware of the trouble he was getting himself into, but that didn't stop him. Grabbing a bottle of water, he sat alone. He hadn't expected Ravi to come and sit by him. Sameer had barely taken a sip and was biting his nails.

Sameer hadn't noticed as Ravi kept rambling to him.

'Hello?! Sameer?'

'Sorry,' Sameer sighed. 'What's up?'

'You, my friend, are stressed.'

'I'm totally fine,' Sameer replied, rolling his eyes.

In the middle of the conversation, Sameer finally saw what he had been waiting for. The group of bullies had gathered around their target for the day. Sameer got up, silently treading to where a crowd had now gathered. He wasn't very shocked to see that they were bullying the short kid he shared some classes with.

The chants of 'Fight, Fight, Fight' fueled the youngster with anger and desire for revenge. It was most likely that the leader of the group had shoved the victim towards another bully. Sameer noticed that if the boy didn't panic, he could easily make use of his height to escape through the circle that had formed around him.

Sameer fought his way through the crowd, pushing his way into the group and stood by the poor boy. With his newly found self-confidence, Sameer yelled, 'You want to fight? I'm up for it.'

By this time, Ravi had joined Sameer. The gang of bullies and Sameer's new gang, comprising of himself, the short boy and Ravi, stood face to face. By now, a hundred 'ooohs' were emanating from the crowd.

'Who do you think you are, huh?' the leader said tauntingly, chuckling with the rest of the group. He again pushed the short boy towards the ground.

Sameer realized that words wouldn't suffice for the awful group. Ravi, who had been standing still the whole time, now did what Sameer couldn't, and pushed one of the bullies.

The crowd was dead silent and no one dared to move — except for the bullies themselves, of course. Shockingly, the group retreated without another word. After making sure that the bullies had left, a round of applause erupted from within the crowd.

Ravi and Sameer were taken aback when they suddenly found themselves being hoisted up by the crowd. Everyone was cheering for them.

Realizing the situation, Sameer was happy to have

helped out and was proud of himself; he was sure his annoying friend was, too.

Sameer knew that the bullies wouldn't change their ways, but at least they wouldn't dare to ever visit this part of the campus again. Hopefully.

After a short while, the boys were put down. Sameer was grateful for the fact that despite the celebratory noise, the headmaster hadn't come out to give them detention.

He took a quick glance at his watch, only to realize that in just a few minutes, he had another class. Motioning with his hands, he told Ravi that he was off to class. Ravi, on the other hand, was still not out of his happy daze, and shrugged his shoulders, continuing with the celebrations.

Sameer was afraid that along with his new friend, he would be called to the headmaster's office. But he couldn't care less. Whatever happened was only fair.

English class wasn't quite exciting — plain old reading of a chapter and an oral discussion. The remaining classes included Chemistry, Sameer's favourite science. Chemistry classes normally took place in the science laboratory for middle graders. Every day, the same routine was followed. A chapter was thoroughly discussed in the first half of the period and during the rest of it, experiments were conducted in pairs. Sameer usually didn't care about who he was partnered with, since he was always engrossed in the task given. Most of the time, his partners wouldn't even help him and instead, just stared at the wall. Sameer was only thankful for that, as he didn't need anyone messing up his experiment. There was this control freak in him that wanted independence in everything. This time, though, his partner was Ravi. They both chatted throughout and messed up the experiment twice. Eventually though, they got it done.

The students were all given enough chemicals to repeat the experiments thrice. Since the boys worked in pairs, the rations were quite perfectly measured. The current exercise included studying the reactions of zinc with sulphuric acid. The small zinc shavings were carefully put inside three separate petri dishes. Ravi was holding the flask of diluted sulphuric acid and observing its water-like appearance.

'Why doesn't it look like acid?' Ravi asked out aloud.

'Because...' Sameer began, but soon got busy preparing the spirit lamp and writing his measurements in the notebook.

'Because *what*, your highness?' Ravi prompted in his trademark sarcastic style.

'Well, what did you think it would look like?'

'Hey, I expected it to be something colourful, something interesting to look at maybe?'

'What, did you expect rainbows and mermaids to be floating in it?'

'Yeah, I really did,' Ravi rolled his eyes, 'the miniature ones.'

Sameer only shook his head and chuckled. 'I get what you mean, but this is a diluted acid, not a concentrated one, so it's going to be far from interesting.'

'You know, I heard that the natural way of getting sulphuric acid is to secure it through collecting acid rain, whenever it happens.' Ravi was being a show-off.

'That's actually wrong, there is no natural way to get sulphuric acid—it has to be made in a lab and all. But yes—acid rain does contain sulphuric acid and it is collected to study the composition and amount of sulphur and nitrogen in it.'

'How would anyone know if it's acid rain or plain old rain?'

'Frankly, you and I wouldn't know. But chemical tests can tell us that. It's the pollution, you know. The molecules of sulphur and nitrogen in the atmosphere react with the water and produce acid rain. Most of the times, the acid in such rain is sulphuric.'

'Hmmmm, interesting!'

'Yes. Isn't it? It was first discovered by Jabar bin Hayan in the eighth century.'

'Oh god, don't start on the Chemistry book's chapter number 1 now, please. That is enough information before the experiment.'

Sameer wasn't too pleased with Ravi's snarky comment. He stared at the reference book, written by the brilliant Larry Joseph, before responding, 'You're just jealous.' Joseph, the lab assistant, was now at their table.

'Is there a problem, folks?' he asked in a friendly voice.

'Yes, Sir.' Ravi put the flask of the acid down on the table. Joseph checked their progress, but they hadn't made much of a headway.

'Why aren't you guys starting on it?'

'Well, we were just wondering...' Sameer started, but Ravi rolled his eyes at him.

'Yes?' Joseph asked helpfully.

'Why aren't we given lab gloves to perform this reaction?'

'You can pull them out of the drawer,' Joseph said with a smile.

'Okay...' Sameer said thoughtfully as Ravi pulled out the rubber gloves and tried them on.

'I didn't know we had the drawer to ourselves,' Sameer said rather sheepishly.

'Actually, I would have laid them out, if you had needed the gloves,' Joseph said, starting to walk away.

The boys stared at him. 'Why *wouldn't* we need them?'

'The acid is a diluted one. We are not giving out concentrated acid to the students. At least, not junior ones.'

Sameer followed Joseph, 'So the seniors would have it?'

'Kid, just go do the experiment,' Joseph chuckled.

Sameer traced his steps back to the table where Ravi

had already placed the zinc shavings inside the beaker. He asked Sameer if he wanted to do the rest of the experiment, but Sameer told him to complete it on his own and offered to take the readings for him. Putting on the gloves, Ravi carefully grabbed the bottle of acid and poured some over the shavings.

'They are supposed to turn into a white salt,' he said as both looked at the glass beaker.

'They're changing colour,' Sameer observed and wrote this in his notebook.

'Yes, but that's not a salt,' Ravi was disappointed.

'Pour some more acid,' Sameer suggested, and Ravi did so. The metallic shavings inside the beaker had turned a rusty brown colour, but that was all.

'Wait, why is it turning brown? Ugh, we are officially the worst at Chemistry.'

'We need to let it dry, I suppose,' Ravi said.

'Or maybe,' Sameer paused, 'we must add some real sulphuric acid to it.'

'They gave us FAKE acid?' Ravi almost shrieked, making the rest of the boys jump out of their skins.

'Shush!' Joseph said from his desk.

'Hold your horses,' Sameer hissed at Ravi. 'It's not fake…it's just not real,' he added.

'Wow! And that is the best explanation of the century,' Ravi rolled his eyes again.

Sameer ignored him and walked towards Joseph. 'Could we have a little concentrated acid?'

'Forget it,' Joseph said, already beating himself up for telling this detail to a very curious kid.

'What I want is results. Like, real results.'

'You are getting results. Allow the acid to evaporate and the shavings shall be fluffier, like a heap of powdered salt. Or almost like it.'

'So there is no hope, ever?' Sameer pulled a face.

Joseph looked at him briefly, and said, 'Maybe, if you earn it.'

Joseph went to check on all the boys who were done with their experiments and took a look at their findings. Sameer, along with Ravi, performed the experiment once again, while wondering how he could earn the right from Joseph.

FOUR

The last period of the day at Kingston High was the Activity Club for the eighth graders. This included the Drama Club, Horseback Riding Troupe, the Gymnastic Band, Art and Handiwork and the Football Team. These activities took place from two in the afternoon. If the coaches were kind, they would let them off at four or four-thirty. Otherwise, a three-hour session would make up for the rest of the day that the boys had spent cooped up in the classrooms. There would, however, be a practical test at each term end, of the students' skills of whatever activity they had chosen. The boys were to choose between the usual field games including hockey, football and horse riding; or they could focus on the wide range of martial arts that the school offered. Sameer's focus was the football team, of which he was the co-captain. Every time he thought of his lucky stars, he felt giddy. It was an amazing feeling, one that made him understand the phrase, 'Cloud nine.'

His favourite thing about the last period was that there were no strict teachers monitoring them, and the sports coaches were very friendly, so chances of a nervous reaction would also be less. Sameer was always glad to see his teammates on the field or in the changing rooms, perked up, like himself, for the practice session every day.

Now that Sameer had taken up the additional responsibility of being co-captain, he felt more conscious of his conduct and presence on the field than before. He had sensed that Faizan, the captain, and Rauf, the previous co-captain, were best buddies. They both did not seem quite happy with the fact that Sameer, a newcomer, had replaced Rauf so quickly. They did not shake hands with Sameer before the game began or even acknowledge his presence. When Sameer had gone up to them to say hi, they responded coldly. While he had made new friends, he had picked up a few enemies too. Sameer decided to ask the coach later to make his teammates work out together, either at the gym or the field, so that they could all be together when prepping for the game.

When it came to working out, Sameer didn't really have a specific routine, believing that workouts had to be changed every few days. That day, he started off with punching bags, where he met Ravi. The two practised on the bags for a good one hour. Sneakily, they decided to indulge in a quick boxing fight. They both, however, ended up with bruised knuckles and a lesson for the day—never defy rules again.

Sameer and Ravi both had swollen hands and aching

arms but they still pushed each other to complete the rest of the workout.

'Listen, you can feel free to do my share, too, what say?' Ravi panted as he dropped on the floor like a rag doll.

'Get up, Ravi, we have this under control,' the self-determined Sameer clenched his jaw when he lifted the dumbbells.

Ravi grumbled and got up to do the same weights, but before he could complain again, Sameer felt the energy drain from his legs. He glanced towards Ravi who was being very brave about his exercise routine.

'I think we can call it a day...' Sameer started.

Ravi looked at his friend's face and dropped the weights immediately.

'See? I told you! Good thinking, Sameer!' Ravi exclaimed, walking towards the exit and raced out. Sameer laughed at his friend's hurried escape, as he too headed towards the hostel.

After a long day, Sameer went back to his dorm room to rest, only to be reminded of another test the day after. He thanked his lucky stars when he learnt of a group study session for the same test in the neighbouring dorm. He gathered his books, notebook, sachet of ready-to-drink cocoa and an empty mug, hoping his neighbours could get him some hot water.

Sameer had not yet met the student who had invited him over. He had assumed it would be a huge number of people in a prefect's dorm room. But when he went there, he felt stupid.

Of course, who else would it be besides his fool of a friend who would want entertainment even while studying for a test? Sameer entered his friend's dorm and saw what he'd already suspected—a very messy room. Not that he could judge too much; his own did not look very tidy either.

Sameer rolled his eyes and laughed at Ravi. Though he couldn't say that they studied thoroughly, he could sincerely say that he and the other boys had one of the best times of their lives since having moved to Kingston. After finishing their revision, the students managed to spare some time for a game of 'Never Have I Ever'—Ravi's idea. Obviously.

'I'll go first!' Ravi said excitedly.

'No, me please,' Babar interrupted.

Ravi frowned, but let it go, 'Go ahead.' He finished making the 'I Have' and 'I Have Never' signs and handed them out to each of the seven players.

Babar continued, 'Never have I ever played the guitar.'

Sameer hesitantly turned his sign around to 'I Have' with all the boys staring at him with wide eyes.

Ravi raised his eyebrows, 'Why do *I* not know of this?' he was surprised.

Sameer only shrugged his shoulders.

'Wait a minute, any chance you have a guitar lying

around in your dorm?' Babar questioned.

Sameer quickly shook his head.

'Sorry, but your expressions gave it away,' Ravi muttered and raced for the door, while Sameer was left clutching his head—it was his bad luck that Ravi knew the way to his dorm room too.

Ravi soon returned and shoved the guitar into Sameer's hands, and then squinted as if in deep thought, 'Hmm, I think I want you to play—'

'What makes you think I'm going to play in front of you all?' Sameer interrupted meekly.

'Because you will, okay?'

Babar chipped in too, 'Bro, you should be so proud of yourself if you can play the guitar. It's an accomplishment!'

The group started cheering Sameer on, until he finally gave in, and started strumming. He realized the wonders of a shared cup of hot cocoa: opening up to each other and making friends for life.

♪

Sameer had been tremendously appreciative of his parents for getting him admitted to the best boys' school in his area. His mom had told him that a great great grandfather of his had been on the board of governors when the British had founded the school in the 1800s. He had always wanted to ask his parents why he had to live within the school premises. He had assumed they were sick of him, though he was continuously reassured by his mother that it was a ridiculous thought.

Thinking of his parents also reminded him of his younger twin sisters. He didn't realize how much he missed them until he had been away from home for less than a week. Sameer sometimes wished that he had an older brother studying at Kingston with him. That way, he'd have company while performing his bizarre chemical experiments and even someone to guide him.

For the first few weeks, he had felt isolated from everyone. But now thanks to Ravi, he hopefully wouldn't have to feel the same way in the next few years to come. Sameer had talked to his mother the night before. Just before disconnecting, he had even talked to his dog on Skype. His mother laughed at him, but Sameer was well aware that Pepper understood each and every thing he said.

The part of the session involving daily routine tests was over. Time was passing quicker than ever, now that he had adjusted.

It was a Thursday, and Sameer wanted to have a well-rested, relaxed day. It was tough not to constantly stress about his studies, considering that he was living right inside the school.

FIVE

Sameer had recently downloaded a programme on his laptop, which would help him learn a new language. He had learnt from the senior boys that in the next couple of years, they would have to learn a foreign language. The options were limited to Spanish, Chinese, Hindi and German.

'Oh, that is why there is a handful of Chinese, Indian and German teachers and students sprinkled all around the campus,' he had exclaimed in a moment of eureka. They were all part of an exchange programme.

'Yep,' the seniors had chirped in. If you score the highest in the language, you get a straight ticket to that country as an exchange student.'

'What are you studying?'

'*Deutsche Sprache, Herr,*' the senior had replied with an accent and in a language that sounded made up.

'What?' Sameer scrunched up his nose.

The boys let out peals of laughter.

'German, my dear boy,' the older boys had ruffled his hair and gone away laughing, probably making fun of him.

Sameer had thought about it. If at all, he would like

to go to Spain, the land of bullfighting and Antonio Banderas. He had been a diehard fan of the actor and one of his favourite movies was *The Mask of Zorro*. As a young boy, he had always worn a black cape and a mask for his fancy dress shows, and when someone mistook him for Batman, he would get angry and take it as an insult.

Sinking into his bed, he opened the programme, and then clicked on the language 'Spanish'. He had been trying to get a chance to learn and speak the language fluently ever since he had heard it as a kid.

Sameer spent more than an hour on his laptop, too engrossed in understanding the basics. He hadn't noticed that even when he wasn't on the campus, he still spent the rest of his time learning something or the other.

The students weren't normally allowed into the school's premises after five in the evening, so the silent dorms, even his own friend's, intrigued him. His curiosity led him to think of all the upcoming school events. This, in turn, reminded him of the ones right around the corner—the surprise school trip and the seniors' farewell party.

The boys, including Sameer, were all annoyed by the fact that the principal had announced a surprise trip, but the location and date had not been revealed and it was almost two weeks that the boys had been held in suspense.

The teenage boys had been awaiting this very moment for the longest time. The excitement had run through the school like a shot of adrenaline, so much so that the boys had forgotten all about staying mad at the school management. The confirmed news about the trip spread swiftly and contagiously soon after it had been announced by the principal's office. Ravi had been the most excited; he had managed to stand up on the teacher's chair to frantically yell at the top of his voice, 'I told you something was cooking in the staff room, didn't I?'

'Yeah, yeah,' Sameer replied to him softly, 'You are the psychic, duh.' He looked back at the boisterous crowd and saw that the rest of the class showed a mix of emotions: excitement, disgust, boredom and indifference. The extroverts were thrilled, the intelligent ones couldn't care less—they probably knew anyway, as they were part of the student council—and the backbenchers finally straightened up on their chairs as soon as the announcement had boomed through the corridors.

The boys had been so caught up in the news of the school trip, that they had even forgotten the main part. The place they were supposed to be visiting was still unannounced, not that the students cared a lot about the location. Anywhere they had a chance to be free and gossip continuously was okay with them.

Later in the day, the school boarders had been

lucky enough to be informed that the trip was to the Hiran Minar, built in honour of Mughal king Jahangir's pet antelope. The kids would get to visit the city of Sheikhupura, a city close to Lahore, where the school was. The day-students had been informed of the news a day later via text message.

A confirmation notice for the trip to the Hiran Minar was sent to the parents, asking for their permission. While the principal would set different locations for each grade, this time it had been collectively agreed upon by the staff that the Hiran Minar would be a perfect learning experience for boys of all ages. And since the main focus of all history lessons would be about the Mughals, it was an advantage for the boys to learn in depth about one of the greatest emperors.

SIX

'Almost forgot it!' Sameer tilted the guitar to show Ravi what he was referring to. Thanks to his friends, he had gotten over his shyness. Just in case the bus ride would become boring, Sameer had brought his guitar to entertain everyone. He was thankful for being permitted to take such a valuable item to the Hiran Minar. In all the excitement, they had almost missed the bus. 'We made it!' The boys had exclaimed upon hopping into the bus. The teachers glared at them. Now, Sameer just had to be very responsible.

Although it was the day of the school trip, the boys weren't as loud as they were on the day of the announcement. The news had finally sunken in. They realized that they were going to a minar for the dead pet of King Jahangir, and now weren't too thrilled about it at all. Still, they had hoped that something interesting would come up, and obviously, they wouldn't want to miss it. Many of the boys would have stayed at the school, if allowed to roam around freely, but they weren't. So anything was better than rotting alone in the dorms of Kingston High.

The ride to Hiran Minar was full of laughter, music and astonishing remarks being made about the wealth of Jahangir. They thought his pet antelope, in whose memory the structure was built, was a rather lucky dude.

A few minutes before the bus came to a stop, the supervising teacher told all the boys to make sure they had brought everything and that it was all sorted. Soon, Sameer realized that his awesomely irresponsible friend had forgotten all of Sameer's precious hazelnut-filled chocolates that the duo had packed for the trip. He remembered Ravi carrying them in a bag, and now they were probably rotting away on a bench somewhere. He couldn't believe Ravi and gave him a good lecture on management and reliability in front of everyone.

'It's a forty-kilometre ride and then a two-hour stay and then a ride back to school. Can you survive through that much deprivation of food? I know I can't!'

Ravi was laughed at. Even the teachers chuckled.

'Hey, I'll let you guys borrow my food!' One of the boys in the bus offered sympathetically, making the others burst into another fit of laughter.

Finally, the bus stopped and the boys hopped out excitedly, yelling and laughing loudly. They were welcomed by the administration and given pamphlets filled with information about the historical and geographical details of the monument. The majority of the pamphlets were stuffed inside the students' backpacks. A tour guide, along with the teachers, was there to guide them anyway.

The teacher in charge of the eighth grade announced very proudly that the administration had convinced the owners of the Minar to let the students take motorboat rides on the man-made lake in the middle of the premises. The tour guide had also informed the students that the eighths were the only lucky grade that was going to get the exclusive boat ride experience.

However, after waiting for a long time, they realized that they were not so 'lucky' anymore, as they were informed that due to some technical problems, they would have to wait for a half hour to ensure the motorboats' safety. During this time, the boys couldn't go anywhere inside the Minar, because the tour guide was unavailable. Sameer and Ravi were jealous of the other groups touring the site already.

The boys became hungrier by the second, and eventually, opened their lunch boxes one after the other as they sat around the garden and began eating. But Sameer and Ravi only looked at one another.

'C'mon, let's get something from the canteen.'

'Yeah…there should be one nearby,' Ravi replied, looking around.

It was evident that none of the boys had done any prep or research on the Hinar Minar, as they were all completely oblivious to the fact that there wasn't any canteen on site.

'Let's ask the teacher,' suggested Sameer, but that was against Ravi's adventurous streak. He pulled at his friend's wrist and tugged him out of their teachers' and classmates' sight. In an attempt to avoid anyone spotting them, they veered away from the concrete path and slipped under a thick cover of trees and bushes. Twigs and leaves from the untamed trees with huge trunks got stuck in their already messy hair. But what they weren't aware of was that they had unknowingly gone into a twisted tunnel. They abruptly stopped in their tracks when Ravi accidently kicked a huge stone, which landed a few feet away from the two. The detail that caught the boys' attention was the stone's symmetrically divided pattern. The pattern had been distinctively divided out into four squares with four different colours. It looked old and faded, but was quite clearly visible.

Sameer's detective instincts kicked in; he pulled out a tissue from his bag and cautiously wrapped it around the stone to pick it up. Who knows, it could be valuable and what not! Confused, he looked at all sides of the stone to see if it was of any importance. He figured that their time wasn't necessarily being wasted, when soon enough, Ravi found a sentence carved into the back of the stone, in cursive handwriting. He pointed it out to Sameer. The boys were bewildered and read it out together:

To the north of the memory, lies the secret.

'Um, well don't ask me, I have a really bad memory,' Ravi raised his hands as if in defeat.

Sameer scoffed, 'You're an idiot.'

'Why, thank you!'

'Shut up, let me think,' Sameer responded quietly, in deep thought, 'the Minar was built in the antelope's memory.' His friend had realized that too, his eyes widening.

'But what does that mean...exactly?' Ravi questioned, while Sameer silently pondered over the same.

He steadily jogged towards the Minar and unsurprisingly, didn't see any of the other boys. They were still touring the garden. He figured out the north of the Minar and saw nothing but an abandoned cabin-like place that might have belonged to some caretaker many years ago. Sameer was almost about to turn around and give up, but Ravi encouraged him to go on.

'You want to go check it out?'

'Why not?' Sameer agreed to his friend's idea, as the two helped each other climb up the tall, rusty gates that made the place look like an abandoned sanitarium.

Upon entering, the boys saw an old, deserted garden and the small cabin. It seemed like it could hardly fit two rooms. The door was heavy and creaked as the boys pushed it open. Dust, cobwebs and bird poop were the only adornments inside. When the boys finally got in, they didn't know what to do. They had arrived at the 'north of the memory', but Sameer found it impossible to find out anything else without further clues. The cupboards could be searched for clues, he thought.

One important feature that did not immediately catch his attention was a huge painting on the wall with some kind of typescript on it. It was roughly four feet in length and two feet in width.

'It is enormous!' said Ravi.

'Is this some kind of a magic spell?' Ravi was totally in the Indiana Jones mode.

'My genius bro, it is Persian verses.'

'Well, read them, then!'

'I can read them out, but I don't understand Persian!'

'Ask Google,' Ravi suggested and that idea sounded good to Sameer.

He took out his phone and typed the eight lines to translate them into English. Thankfully, Internet connection was available.

Sameer abruptly stopped speaking and looked up. He couldn't make out the last word and to the boys' disappointment, that portion was covered by some sort of a liquid that was now probably stuck to it forever. Ravi walked over to the painting and hopelessly attempted to scratch out the residue with a broken twig he had picked up from the floor.

In his vigorous attempts to find out what the word was, he poked the painting too hard and the already loose tacks that were holding it up, snapped, making the painting first wobble, and then fall down with a crash. It had shattered to pieces.

The boys were flabbergasted. Horror was written all over their faces, as they thought they would get into serious trouble for what they had done. Sameer held his head in dismay, looking down at the floor. Ravi, though, chose to look upwards, seeking divine help.

However, they were in for a surprise.

The painting and the verses were nothing but a distraction, for right behind them was a tightly fastened window whose frame was visible, but there was no latch or handle to open it! Ravi looked at Sameer, who was still looking down, mourning the loss of the painting. Ravi, too astounded to speak, shook him by the shoulder. Irritated, Sameer looked up at him and opened his mouth to yell, but Ravi pointed towards the wall with both hands.

'Lookie here, Sameer!' he exclaimed.

'Wow!' Sameer said, instantly forgetting all about the painting.

Sameer took the stick from Ravi, gripped it firmly and poked the frame of the window.

'There must be a latch,' he said after poking the window from all angles.

'Where?' Ravi was also feeling for it all around the window.

The boys looked around for a latch, a switch or a

button, but there was nothing. The walls were solid rock and nothing else.

'Let's try pushing it,' Ravi suggested.

'Okay, but let's be gentle.' Sameer was not yet fully out of the trauma of the broken painting. Whatever it was, a disguise or not, it was heritage. Luckily, the wooden frame and the painting itself, made on some sort of leather, was intact and could be mended.

Ravi and Sameer both pushed the window, gently at first and then a little harder. The wall did not budge. Their collective huffing and puffing just blew out sand from the crevices of the frame.

'It's of no use,' Sameer said. But Ravi thought differently. He gave the wall around the frame a sharp nudge and it creaked, moving inwards a little. Sameer became alert, and both threw their weight against the wall, pushing with both hands.

The wall eventually caved in, revealing a tunnel that was two-feet deep.

They looked at each other, half intrigued, half scared. The excitement of revealing a mystery was greater than the fear of some bogeyman that could reach out and pull them inside the wall, torture them and later maybe eat them up for dinner.

'Is it going to be me?' Sameer asked Ravi.

'What? To go in?'

'Yeah,' Sameer said drily.

'By all means. I will follow you,' Ravi said promptly.

'Chicken,' Sameer muttered.

'Chicken who?' Ravi was hurt. 'Let me go then!' He pushed past Sameer and before anything could be said or done, he slid through the tunnel like a swift lizard and was gone in the dark. Sameer watched him with his mouth hanging open. He heard a small thud a few seconds later and called out, 'Hey, Ravi, you okay, buddy?'

There was no reply. Sameer thrust his body inside the opening, reaching as far as he could go, while keeping his feet on the ground. He wanted to be able to run and ask for help if needed. His mouth went dry when he didn't hear a reply.

It was pitch dark. 'Ravi, you there?' Sameer asked louder.

'Err, yeah,' a faint sound reached him.

'Oh my god! Are you alright?'

'I guess. It is horribly dark out here, that's all,' Ravi shouted. Overjoyed, Sameer jumped into the tunnel and landed with a dull thud.

Sameer turned on his phone's torch so they could see where they were.

They were surrounded by huge rolls of leather. At first, the boys thought these were newspapers and that they had been pranked. But soon they discovered that they were old, stained scrolls written by Emperor Jahangir himself, according to the stamps at the bottom right corner of the pages.

'Well...' The boys didn't know what to say.

'This is unbelievable,' Sameer and Ravi chanted at once.

'It is amazing, out of this world, fantabulous!'

'Do you think we must take these to the teachers?' Sameer thought out aloud. 'What will they say?'

Ravi too, thought out loud, 'Well, they will yell, for sure.'

'But then they will also be proud of us!'

'So, worth the risk?'

'Absolutely, definitely.'

So it was decided. Ravi bent over and Sameer climbed atop his back, crawled through the tunnel and climbed out through the window. He had also taken Ravi's shirt with him. Once out, he took off his own shirt, and tied the sleeves together to make a makeshift rope. He leaned into the window and dropped the full length of the rope to his friend. After a few strenuous minutes of pulling, and much sweat and tears, the duo was once again standing on the same ground. They put on their stained shirts, clutched two of the rolls that Ravi had brought up with him and ran towards the lake.

On the way, running and panting, Sameer asked him if he could smell something.

'Fooooood!' he yelled.

Sameer laughed at his friend as the two boys ran non-stop and reached the lake. Their jaws fell open upon seeing that their classmates were still waiting to do the course of the motorboats and the teachers were doing a headcount, asking where two boys had vanished.

'We are right here,' Sameer walked up to them. They all looked relieved, but suddenly wore an expression of anger when they asked where the boys had been off to. Sameer and Ravi had quite a story to tell the teachers, who refrained from saying anything to the rest of the students. Later, when the one of the caretakers of the Hiran Minar came to tell them that it was time to close the monument, the teachers informed him about the scrolls. Sameer, Ravi, the teachers and the other students were taken to the strange cabin where a score of these scrolls were lying in the basement. A member of the caretaking staff climbed down, packed up all the scrolls, and brought them back with him. He told them that the administration would take them into custody.

The two boys were then given a lecture by the teachers about how reckless they had been, but the rest of the boys started cheering for them.

'Hip, Hip, Hurray!'

'Cheers for Sameer!'

'Cheers for Ravi!'

The teachers smiled faintly. The boys looked at them and knew the scolding was over. Sameer played his guitar in the bus on the way back, entertaining the kids as well as the teachers. Ravi danced to the music despite the fact that he looked like a chicken and the song he was dancing to was a very sad one.

'What a day!' Ravi said to Sameer.

'Bloody brilliant!' Sameer winked. They high-fived each other and said good night before going towards their dorms, tired from the day's adventure

∽

The next day, the principal announced in the school assembly that the scrolls had been verified by the Lahore Heritage Museum, and it would mention their names as well as the school's, on the display plaque in the section for Mughal History. Ravi and Sameer jumped with joy and felt very proud.

SEVEN

Sameer had been listening to his favourite music when Ravi barged into his room, 'Are you ever going to stop embarrassing me?'

'What?' Sameer was confused.

'I have an image to maintain,' Ravi said in a very regal tone.

'Oh dear god,' Sameer sighed and threw his head back in mock disbelief.

'This party is something I have been looking forward to all my life—'

Sameer cut him off in between. 'All your life? Even when you hadn't come to Lahore to study at Kingston?'

'The point is—' Ravi began, ignoring his best friend's sarcasm.

'What, what is the point?' Sameer cut in.

'I am coming to it!' said Ravi.

'Well, I don't have all day,' Sameer was enjoying the frustration of his friend.

'The point is, Sameer, that you have no personality,' he pulled a face.

'You beast!' Sameer was not expecting such a turn of events.

Ravi, who had been standing all this while, was rolling on the floor with laughter.

'Self-loving maniac,' Sameer was hurling remarks at him and Ravi just laughed. Once they were done, Ravi actually told him what the problem was.

'You need to pull your act together, Sameer. In the looks department, you know,' he sounded so serious that Sameer broke into laughter once again.

'You are such a naïve little boy,' said Sameer.

Ravi pulled a face.

'I am alright,' said Sameer confidently.

'Yeah, but "alright" isn't going to make an impression, you know, my dear Sir. We need to make an impression on the audience. That is what I worry about.'

Sameer forced a smile and tried to make sense of what his friend was so worried about. 'Where is this audience, Ravi?'

'The school party! How could you forget?'

'Of course I haven't forgotten. I know there is a party. The costumes, the decoration, the hullaballoo make it quite difficult for me to forget there is a party coming up.' Despite trying hard, Sameer could not help his frustration.

'Why are you such a spoilsport? Why? Why did you have to be my friend in all of this world?' Ravi was clearly disappointed in his best buddy.

'Listen up, I hear there is a competition for putting

up the best trick. I know there are going to be lots of people vying for that prize,' Sameer said, trying to sound interested.

'And I am not among them, Sameer.'

Sameer could see that it was not a joke anymore. The competition really mattered a lot to Ravi. It was his job to stick with him and be his biggest support. 'I will do my best to come up with a good trick,' he said in a promising tone.

'Yes!' Ravi said excitedly. 'But that is not what I am worried about...' he said in a thoughtful way.

Oh god, Sameer thought.

'It's your...' Ravi stopped midway.

Sameer checked himself in the mirror. He was all right. He was a little upset that his friend did not find him presentable enough to attend a party.

'Not your face, stupid!'

'Then what? You're being mean,' Sameer felt hurt.

'No, just your casual way of dressing up. *That's* a put-off, Sameer. Here I shall be all dressed up like a Hollywood star in a suit and tie and you shall insist on your jeans and tee.'

'Those are my comfy clothes!'

'Well, your "comfy clothes" are seriously not cool!'

'Hollywood stars wear jeans and tees!'

'Not my kind of Hollywood stars!'

'Gosh!'

'See?'

'What?'

'You ran out of arguments.'

'Whatever. I am not arguing anymore.'

'Good. Ask your mum to send over a suit, a crisp white shirt and a tie for you. ASAP.'

'I have one, you idiot.'

'Really? Good then. Problem solved!' Ravi grinned ear-to-ear and vanished from the room as suddenly as he had entered.

The theme of the party was 'SPOOKY'. Sameer wasn't interested at all, and honestly, the theme scared him. Considering the school was enormous, anything and everything could go wrong, though he hoped nothing would. Sameer would've tried and convinced at least his friend to not participate in the decorating sessions, but at the moment all he could do was sit and procrastinate. He had already done his bit by taking part in the decorations and did not have much more to offer.

Sameer checked the date on his laptop. It was the 25th of October. He could hear some shrieks from down the hall. Some boys had come back to their dorms after their turns at the decoration, and some were day-scholars, who had gotten special permission from their parents to stay back after school hours to help the boarders with the prep. Since he had nothing important to do for the rest of the evening, Sameer thought he might as well head down to the campus to see to see what the boys had accomplished. He had seen the decorations before he came to the dorm, and they were gaudy, tacky, but absolutely what they had planned them to be—spooky!

Upon entering the campus, Sameer saw students engrossed in preparing for the party. The juniors were carving pumpkins and Sameer was amused watching his friend do the same. His attention moved over to the artsy students who were painting the walls, while some were making masks and even costumes for sale. Sameer went over to have a look at them, but boy, were they steeply priced or what!

Sameer started feeling differently about the event now. It seemed to only be some sort of a costume contest. It looked harmless, and no one seemed to be preparing pranks. This gave Sameer more reasons to mull over his decision to not attend the party.

'What could go wrong?' Sameer mumbled, before going to meet his friend. Ravi could definitely use some help. If not that, some company could always help.

Sameer and Ravi didn't do much other than cracking simple jokes and laughing their heads off. The same pattern continued for a half hour, until from a distance, Sameer noticed some cooking going on in the hostel's kitchenette.

'I'll be right back,' Sameer said to his friend, and strolled over to the stall. Creepy-looking desserts were being prepared by the kitchen staff here. This is better than all that decoration, Sameer thought. He understood why the desserts were being prepared beforehand; the next morning would be super busy. The teachers and students would have to attend school during the day.

Sameer looked hungrily at the desserts and saw someone watching him from behind the service window. He tried to see from the corner of his eye, but couldn't recognize who it was. So, he looked up to see that the watchful pair of eyes belonged to the chef's assistant; a boy of around sixteen, thin and frail. He didn't look like someone who worked in the kitchen, for the two chefs who prepared the meals were as round as cauldrons.

'You want some?' the boy asked Sameer.

'Er, no. Thanks.' Sameer wasn't a greedy boy.

'Yeah, I couldn't give you any either. The chef counts them and writes them on a board on the wall,' the boy said, shuddering at the thought of stealing.

'You work here?' Sameer asked him.

'Yes, the evening shift. Have to go to school in the morning.'

'You mean here?'

'Oh no! Not here. The other school, down the road.'

Sameer looked confused.

'It is a public school,' the helper added.

'Oh,' Sameer said and immediately wished he hadn't.

'What is your name?' Sameer asked him.

'Asim,' the boy replied. 'And you are Sameer, aren't you?'

'How do you know?'

'Well, I watched the game the other day.'

'You did? You like football?'

'Oh yes, I have started a team in my school as well. I call it Asim 11.'

'Haha, that is super!'

'Well, I got to get back to work. You must run along too,' Asim suggested.

'Yeah, I guess.'

'Or…' Asim took his words back while Sameer waited for him to continue, 'I'm nearly done. You want to go visit my school?' Asim had just finished his job of placing the washed and dried utensils inside their respective drawers and cabinets.

'For real?' Sameer asked, for he had never thought he was one of those kids who could sneak out of school. He had always played by the rules. He thought about it for a moment and then the boredom of the daily routine nudged him into saying, 'Ok, um…sure.'

'Okay, let's go.' Asim was very keen to get out of the boarding school's kitchen and back to his own school.

'Wait, let me grab my friend real quick,' Sameer had to bring along his partner-in-crime so that if they got caught, they would have each other's company in detention!

Asim looked uncomfortable, 'Which friend?'

Sneaking out with too many boys of Kingston High could get him into bigger trouble than Sameer and his friend.

Sameer looked at Asim thoughtfully. He kind of understood the dilemma Asim was going through. 'Don't worry at all about Ravi. He can keep a secret. I would vouch for him more than I would vouch for me,' Sameer put a hand on Asim's shoulder to reassure him.

'Sure,' Asim replied briefly. Sameer's face lit up. He had not had such a rush of emotions since the discovery at the Hiran Minar. The same routine not just bored him, but also made it difficult for him to study properly. Sameer was a restless soul. He needed to escape from reality every few days to keep his adventurous streak satisfied. He knew he was bending the rules, but the curiosity to see the working of a public school in comparison to his posh private school got the better of him.

Sameer swiftly jogged over to Ravi where he was showing off his costume for the party.

'Hey, Ravi, gather your stuff and come with me!' Ravi and Sameer were the kind of friends who trusted each other and did not have to ask a lot of questions. They both bid adieu to the boys who had gathered around.

'What in the world are you doing?' Sameer asked him, eyebrows furrowed.

'I, my friend, am going to be Mr Handsome at the

end of the party,' Ravi jutted out his chin as if he was going to be crowned Prince Charming right at that moment. Sameer grabbed his head with both his hands as he silently chuckled.

'What are the odds of that though?' Ravi was quite serious.

'Zero,' Sameer chuckled loudly and Ravi sulked. 'Jealous,' he hissed in his friend's ear and they both punched each other jokingly.

'So...?' Ravi said.

Sameer realized he had been leading his friend towards the kitchen without even telling him what was going on. 'Asim and I are going to go visit his school that's down the road,' Sameer said as if it was no big deal.

'Who in the freaking world is Asim?' Ravi was quizzed.

'The kitchen assistant,' Sameer replied.

'Is this a joke?' Ravi stopped in his tracks and stared at his friend in disbelief.

'No, and it's going to be super fun,' Sameer said in a matter-of-fact tone and kept walking towards the kitchen.

'Listen, buddy, I have no intention of standing in the headmaster's office with my mother yelling down my ear cavity through the phone all the way from India, "This is not what I sent you there for!"'

Sameer looked at his friend thoughtfully. 'Nothing

will happen,' he said reassuringly.

'Have you done it before?'

'We will be back in an hour, max!'

'It's not that I don't want to go,' Ravi said longingly.

'I know! And that is why you must. I promise you, we will be back in one hour.'

Ravi shrugged and started walking. They reached the kitchen where Asim was already waiting for them. The boys exchanged greetings and fist bumps.

'So, what now?' Ravi was the voice of reason among the trio of very adventurous boys.

'I usually leave the building from gate number 1, the one used by the custodian staff, but that is always guarded,' said Asim

'They wouldn't let us pass?' Sameer asked.

'Why would they, Mr Smart?' Ravi said with a smirk.

'We can use gate 2 or 3,' suggested Asim.

'I didn't know there was a gate number 3 in the school,' Sameer was surprised.

'Actually, it is not really a gate. It is a door beside the compound near the on-campus servant's quarters. The gardener, the guards and the cook who stay in these quarters use the door to go outside,' Asim told the boys. Ravi and Sameer exchanged looks, excited at the possibility of successfully escaping school without being caught.

They silently walked with their heads down. The

schoolboys were following the trail of Asim, who had asked them to stay low-key so that they do not get noticed. They reached the servant's quarters. The cabins were all locked, since the guards were on duty. Splashing and showering sounds could be heard from the bathroom that was located just beside the cook's cabin. Maybe the cook was inside. Asim signalled them to hurry.

All three pairs of eyes landed on a small gate that was rustier than the others. It was a golden chance to escape. The boys jogged towards the gate in a line, one behind the other, as if they were part of a serious, life-threatening mission. Sameer was the first one to exit the school building. He dramatically looked towards the sky as if he were in a movie, playing the role of a fugitive who had had his first breath of fresh air after a long time in prison.

'Drama queen!' Ravi chuckled from behind. They both skipped along after Asim, who was walking at a great speed, equally excited to leave the premises of the school.

'How far is it from here?' Ravi was trying to do some mental math. He had been promised one hour and he was trying to calculate how much time was to be spent in 'travelling' and how much in 'sightseeing'.

'Ummmm,' Asim replied in a thoughtful way. Both Sameer and Ravi looked at him, waiting for an answer.

'Well?' Sameer prompted and Asim looked at them both.

'It is just around the corner,' he said. The boys were relieved.

Excited and laughing about nothing in particular, the three boys abruptly came to a stop, shoulders banging into each other's, as Ravi got the hardest hit.

'Owww!'

'Shhhh!' the other two whispered in unison.

'What, no one here's listening to us!'

'Well, this is my school...boys,' announced Asim, pointing at his school building.

The boys had been busy fooling around, and hadn't realized when they had reached their destination. Ravi and Sameer were very intrigued. It was a dark brown building, with bright reddish gates. The walls weren't very tall and the inner area of the school could be seen. Murals, probably made by the students themselves, gave the school a very authentic, artistic vibe. Sameer was held captive by the view. Not even the enormous structure of his own school had caught his interest in this manner.

'Wow,' Ravi said softly.

'Awesome! But... I should've brought my camera,' Sameer whined.

'Oh, don't be upset, just keep the memories in your head,' Asim consoled him.

'Great advice, that,' Ravi said sarcastically.

Asim retorted with a frown, 'Maybe there is a camera in the school somewhere.' His lame response made Ravi stick his tongue out, while Asim had nothing more to say and rolled his eyes at the rather annoying fellow.

'Let's go now!' Sameer mouthed excitedly. He grabbed both the bantering boys by their arms and pulled them towards what he thought to be the main gate.

'Stop, stop, stop, stop, stop, bro! Do you want us all to get kicked out? We have to go from the entrance at the back,' Asim hissed.

Ravi chuckled and muttered, 'Well, I think all of us are going to get expelled today.'

'Fine,' Sameer said softly, 'show us the other entrance, though one thing I know is that unofficial entrances are more heavily guarded.'

'Not ours, as a matter of fact,' Asim responded.

Ravi looked shocked, 'You've sneaked into your own school before?'

'Out, not in. And before you judge me, you did the exact same thing today.'

Clearly, Asim and Ravi did not get along, and this was proven when Ravi was quick to add, 'Unwillingly.'

'Could you two stop being such killjoys?' Sameer butted in.

'And do what?' Ravi snapped at his friend.

Sameer did a slight courtesy like a ballet dancer, before saying, 'Look around...' He said it in a dramatic way, as if they had been brought to some exotic place. The playground was bare. There was no grass, but Asim told them that he, his buddies, as well as the other boys could play cricket, football, hockey, wrestling and even race on the same ground, nonetheless. The rest of the compound was dotted with trees. Most of them looked quite bare, but some of them were laden with fruit, like the mulberry and mango trees. The amaltas, or golden rain tree, also looked splendid. The mulberries were ripe and purple, and littered the ground.

'You want to try some?' Asim asked happily, trying to keep his guests entertained.

'Try, as in, eat them?' asked Sameer innocently.

Asim rolled his eyes at Sameer for asking such an obvious question, and started climbing the tree gracefully, almost as well as a monkey. He had left his slippers on the ground and had used all four limbs to reach the middle of the tree in no time.

'Booyah!' Ravi yelled excitedly. 'You the man, Asim!' He was suddenly super excited. Asim bent a branch with fresh mulberries. Sameer and Ravi greedily picked out a handful. They were as sweet as candies. Sameer watched Ravi and Asim finally get along and smiled. He looked around, and called out to Asim, 'Hey, Asim, what do you guys do for fun around here?'

'You gotta be kidding me, right?' Ravi's eyes were as wide as saucers. 'You mean they need to have more fun than this?'

Apparently, Ravi was thrilled about picking the fruits. He even tried to climb up the tree. Asim was giving him directions on how to tighten his grip on the coarsest part of the branch so as to create enough friction to keep him from slipping.

'Curve your feet to get a grip on the tree,' shouted Asim, as Ravi was constantly sliding down and it was very funny to watch.

THUD.

Ravi fell from the lowest branch as he lost his grip. Asim froze in the higher branches, mouth open and eyes wide. Sameer ran to help his friend get up. Ravi was just lying there, eyes closed.

Sameer shouted, 'Ravi! Ravi! Are you all right?' Ravi didn't answer.

'Oh my god!' whispered Sameer, clutching his head. Asim, like a monkey, had smoothly descended from the tree and shook Ravi by the shoulders.

'AAAARRRGHHHHHHHH!' Ravi suddenly sat up cackling, when he sensed he had created enough tension in the atmosphere.

'You crook!' Sameer and Asim started pummelling him in a friendly manner, and they all laughed, relieved that the 'accident' had been just a prank.

'Don't you give me a heart attack like that, ever again!'

Ravi couldn't stop laughing and Sameer threatened to kill him. Ravi then started running, challenging him to try. For the next few minutes, the three boys ran around in circles, attempting to win the slap challenge.

Later, panting, sweating and dusty, they all sat on the ground, telling each other what a good idea it was to come here.

'I guess, but we must leave now,' Sameer said, looking at his watch.

'Yeah, it is almost time,' Ravi agreed.

'Wait, I haven't even shown you the best part yet!'

'You mean there is more?' Sameer and Ravi said together.

'The best is yet to come, my dear sirs,' Asim spoke with dramatic flair. He got up with a jump and told the boys to follow him. He ran towards the back of the school and stopped in front of an empty room.

It seemed to be newly built as compared to the rest of the school building. Sameer and Ravi wondered how they would enter, as the metal door to the building was locked. But Asim already had a key, which he fished out from his pocket and inserted into the lock. The door opened with a creek and they entered a dark room.

'What is this place?' Sameer asked.

Every single window in the room was covered with black paper, giving the room an eerie glow.

'It is a place you would love to be in Sameer,' Asim was being cryptic. Asim switched on the lights and Sameer and Ravi both were amazed.

'Un-freaking-believable,' Sameer breathed as he saw rows and rows of chemical apparatus lined up against the wall, twelve large tables positioned in groups of four and a small desk at the end of the room.

'Wowza!' Ravi exclaimed.

'This, my friends, is our science laboratory.'

'You are kidding me,' Sameer gasped, a little ashamed for thinking lesser of public schools. The laboratory he was standing in was smaller than the one in his school, but it was fully equipped.

'You guys want to have some fun?' Asim was in a mood to entertain. He was showing off a little, but was very happy to see the rich boys from the elite school being impressed by the world he lived in.

'How are we going to do that?'

'Just watch me...' Asim said with a sly smile.

He opened one of the drawers of a large table and took out some plastic bottles and jars. One had some powder and the other, a transparent liquid.

'Have you guys ever done chemical experiments with cooking ingredients?' Asim smiled as he asked.

'What cooking ingredient?' Ravi scrunched up his nose. Sameer was quiet. He was too thrilled at the prospect of reacting fruits and vegetables with chemicals.

'So, do you get the fruits and veggies from around here?' Sameer asked very enthusiastically.

'What fruits and veggies?' Both Asim and Ravi looked at him, puzzled.

'The ones to be used for the experiments...' Sameer spoke, but regretted as soon as he did since his friends went crazy, laughing their heads off. Sameer was flustered. What was so stupid about the question?

'My brother, kitchen ingredients go way beyond your daily potatoes, tomatoes and onions!' Asim was still laughing.

'Okay so...' Sameer was embarrassed.

'So,' Asim paused, stifling a giggle, 'We do this stuff with simple white vinegar and baking soda!'

Asim got into the game, and Sameer and Ravi were amazed to see the simple boy from the kitchen, who worked so hard to earn a living by washing their dirty dishes from the school canteen, performing complex experiments. Asim was very accurately readying the paraphernalia needed for the experiment. He got a glass flask and a funnel. He then carefully measured 100 millilitres of white synthetic vinegar and poured it into the flask. The other two watched the show in silence. Ravi tried to hold the powder for Asim, but Sameer pulled him back. He wanted only Asim to do the magic, be the man of the moment.

'I cannot bring the scientific scales here,' Asim said sheepishly.

'That's all right,' Sameer said with a smile. 'We don't get to shift ours either,' he added, to make Asim feel at ease.

'Err, so, could you go and weigh this for me?' Asim handed over the bottle with the fine powder to Sameer.

'Sure. What is this, though?'

'It is baking soda. The one we use to bake cakes.'

'Oh, nice! Where are the scales?'

'Over there, at the teacher's desk,' Asim pointed towards the small desk at the end of the room. The scientific scales, a normal weighing scale actually, but much smaller in size and encased in a foot-long and foot-wide glass case, sat silently on the teacher's desk. Sameer was thrilled by the classic weighing scales, which were quite different from the electronic scales they were allowed to use back at their school. He had seen vegetable vendors back home use these scales to measure, and had always found them fascinating.

He carefully poured a certain amount of the powder into one side of the scales and they tipped. Sameer was confused. What happened?

'Did you take the weights from the slot?' Asim asked just at that moment.

Yikes, thought Sameer. 'Uh, yeah, sure!' he answered, turning back to the scales again to see where the slot was.

'Liar,' a voice whispered from behind him and Sameer jumped. He turned back to see a grinning Ravi standing right next to him.

'Shut up.'

Ravi grinned.

'There they are,' Sameer spotted the small shallow slot outside the glass casing, attached to the glass wall of the scales with glue. There were the smallest weights imaginable: 1 gram, 2 grams, 5, 10 and so on.

'I shall need 50 grams of that stuff,' Asim called out again.

'Yeah, I know!' Sameer was feeling like a subordinate. He fished out the weight that had '50 grams' written on it and placed it in the second cup of the scales. Nothing happened.

'You have poured too much powder there, see?' Ravi pointed out.

Sameer picked up the cup with the powder and Ravi held the plastic bottle, while he poured some of the powder back. It took a few trials of adding and subtracting the powder until a perfect balance was created. Sameer carried the cup from the scales to Asim, quite pleased with him himself.

'Tell me that was fun,' Asim said.

'Yep,' Sameer and Ravi said, grinning.

'Well, that was boring actually. What is going to happen *now* is fun. This is the easiest way to create carbon dioxide gas.'

Sameer and Ravi were interested.

'You guys like balloons?' Asim asked cheekily.

'We're not kids,' Ravi said, offended a little.

'Um, yeah but believe me, on your way back to the hostel, you are going to be holding a balloon.' He cackled as he spoke.

Ravi and Sameer exchanged glances and made faces at the silly idea. Asim quietly pulled out a deflated balloon from the desk's drawer. He then poured the weighed amount of baking soda in the flask holding the vinegar. He immediately covered the mouth of the flask with the balloon and right in front of their eyes, the balloon started filling up rapidly. The chemical reaction between the soda and vinegar was making enormous fizzy bubbles in the flask and gassy vapours could be seen floating upwards into the balloon.

A few minutes later, after they had cleaned up, locked the room and jumped over the fence to walk towards the boarding school, the passers-by on the road chuckled to see the teenage boys taking turns to hold a balloon filled with the gas they had themselves created.

EIGHT

The next day, Sameer couldn't wait to see Asim after school hours. He went straight to the kitchen after lunch, when the cook was back at his own cabin and Asim would be working alone. He was in fact prepping for the party. He waited for a moment until Asim started making desserts resembling human fingers and baby pumpkins. These were fairly simple, while Sameer had expected something a little more elaborate. The fingers were made of breadsticks and the nail polish was created using a mix of water and food colour. The baby pumpkins were nothing but spooky faces drawn onto oranges, using a black marker.

Sameer left Asim to his job and walked away from the stall to look for Ravi, who wasn't to be found.

Shrugging, Sameer walked back to his dorm, only to find nothing interesting to do. Instantly, he wished he'd stayed and roamed around the campus. But he didn't feel like going all the way back.

Later at night, Sameer decided to have a quick workout session at the nearby gym. He exercised for quite long and didn't realize that it was getting late. On the way back to his room, his head started aching terribly. Sameer took a quick shower and dozed off.

The next day, he wasn't woken by the bugging sound of his alarm at six in the morning, but by the students chattering and causing a havoc. He knew the excitement had been caused by the pre-party. Checking his clock, Sameer rolled his eyes. It was only five in the morning, while the party was to start no earlier than five in the evening.

An irritated Sameer put on his earphones and tried to go back to sleep, only to wake up half an hour later with another terrible headache. Sameer was surprised that Ravi hadn't come to drag him to participate in the celebrations, considering how pumped up he was for the party. The thought, however, quickly disappeared when the door to Sameer's dorm flung open, scaring him.

'Are you crazy?' Sameer yelled at his friend groggily.

'Maybe,' Ravi shrugged. 'C'mon,' he said, dragging Sameer out of his room and down the stairs, and not even giving him a chance to decide whether he wanted to brush his teeth first or his hair. After Sameer realized the situation, he convinced his friend to at least let him change out of his nightclothes. But Ravi was adamant and dragged his friend to the ground floor.

Sameer rubbed his eyes thoroughly, questioning the sanity of the pupils residing at Kingston. He had no problem with them celebrating if it pleased them, but not at this unearthly hour!

In fact, that day, the school council had called for an early morning meeting to discuss the venue and the prize for the best trick.

It was also annoying that the boys were so enthusiastically celebrating something that wasn't even such a big deal. It probably was for the graduates, but the enthusiasm of the younger kids was confusing. Lost in his thoughts, he wandered past Ravi and reached the main ground. It was so overcrowded that he found it difficult to remember where he was. It was as if he had forgotten all routes inside the school.

It was fifteen past six when the crowd began to thin out. Eventually, Sameer found his way back. He barely had the time to dress up and reached his first class just on time. It was very amusing to Sameer to see the other students act like orangutans, jumping and hooting in class. Their attempts to make scary faces proved to be useless, but of course, they were hilarious.

Sameer would smile at his stupid classmates every now and then. Some, though, seemed as if they had lost all their maturity, senses and manners. Some of the class rebels were also rude to the teachers, despite being punished with detention several times.

Soon, the classes ended and Sameer was still not sure about picking a costume, or even going to the party. Ravi was more than eager about going to the party, for it would be the only occasion where the boys would be allowed to be themselves without much restriction from the school authorities. Some teachers would be on duty, of course, but the students themselves would be the organizers, planners and attendees.

The theme of the party had been carefully chosen, after much debate about whether it should be Star Wars, Harry Potter or Lord of the Rings. It had turned out that everyone liked all three heroes from these series, Darth Vader, Harry Potter and Frodo, and the boys could not pick one out of the three. Thus, they decided to go for a more general theme, Spooky, so that everyone could choose from an array of villains.

Ravi had decided to dress up as the Joker. 'The face paint is easy,' he had excitedly said and the suit was a no-brainer since every student had to keep a suit to wear during occasions, anyway.

Sameer had quietly listened to Ravi's rambles and thought hard about which villain he would want to be. He eventually gave up, considering the whole idea of dressing up too childish.

'You can be Sherlock,' Ravi had suggested.

'Meh,' Sameer drawled.

'Oh yes, we can stick up the collar of your suit with pins, wrap a scarf around this measly neck of yours and get you a hat from one of the stalls the boys have set up.'

'I don't have the whiskers or sideburns,' Sameer challenged him.

'Ah, my boy, do not you worry about your face. I

can only make it look better,' Ravi spoke in the same regal tone that he did when feeling peppy.

'Idiot,' Sameer muttered, and Ravi winked at him, before leaving. 'Sherlock and Joker. We are just too good. No, wait, I am just toooo good!'

Sameer watched him disappear through the entrance and smiled to himself.

I didn't come here to be part of kids' parties anymore, he thought to himself. After having debated with himself about whether or not he would betray his best friend for his own comfort, Sameer had decided, once and for all, that he wasn't going. The cold weather made him plop down on his bed and snuggle beneath the comforter, with his science magazine on his lap. Sameer's mind was blown upon discovering that gallium spoons melted in hot water.

He now felt a pang of guilt for being a spoilsport and a party-pooper for Ravi, who had really been looking forward to this event. There was a knock on the door. It was Ravi, dressed up as the legendary Joker. He mimicked him saying, 'Why so serious?'

To take things up a notch, he even brought a plastic dagger painted in silver and partially smeared with red paint. He looked the real deal.

'Hey, you still not dressed up?' Ravi exclaimed in shock.

'Er, no. Not well,' Sameer lied, in an attempt to save Ravi any heartbreak.

'Oh, bad luck, huh?' he said, hiding his disappointment.

Had this been between girls, they would have plopped some pillows under the sick friend's head, given her some hot beverage, sworn loyalty to the last breath and sat on her side until the she felt better enough to make it to the party. Luckily for Sameer, they were boys.

Ravi turned to go. 'Hey, you okay being on your own, dude?' he asked, concerned.

'Er, yeah, sure. Go enjoy. You look awesome.' Sameer was grateful to Ravi for not noticing how mean he was being.

Sameer had previously thought of calling it an early night and going to sleep, but had given up that idea eventually. The loud noises, shrieks, screams, booms and thuds indicated that no one would be able to sleep before twelve, the curfew. Thankfully, rules had to be followed even during the most celebratory of events.

Every two minutes, the students would be heard chanting in unison, 'Trick or Treat!' Sameer rolled his eyes, as he thought they were a little too old for that. He tried to go back to sleep, but failed yet again. Online hacks and tips proved to be useless or were impossible to do in the school. Anything that Sameer could do to block all noise out was tried without success.

He assumed that at some point before twelve, he

would be tired enough to doze off automatically, but a particular thump and crash caught his attention, primarily because following it, the school quietened for two whole seconds. The interesting fact was that the loud noises resumed right after. It seemed as if the whole school had been possessed for a while, before going back to normal.

Not being able to control his curiosity, Sameer thought to himself that it would be no harm to just check what was happening and come right back up. He didn't have a costume, but he couldn't care less about it at the moment.

Sameer did hear about a 'no costume, no party' rule in school that day and he was even more amused when he heard that it was approved by the headmaster. Thinking no one would actually care enough about him, Sameer, still in his night suit, swiftly walked down the stairs. Surely, he wouldn't be punished for not wearing a costume!

Sameer had expected to see Ravi, though he was grateful his friend wasn't there to interrupt his solo investigation.

He had quickly disappeared into the crowd, shoved mindlessly by fellow students who were all busy having fun. A few metres away from him, he could see firecrackers going off in the sky. On the other hand, Faizan was playing tricks on people. Sameer looked around and thankfully, not too many people frowned at his poor choice of clothes.

There was a group of boys dancing on the left, and on his right, tickets were being sold for a music contest.

Sameer eventually found himself among fewer people and away from the music. It was a blessing, he thought. For the short while he was at the party, he had been enjoying himself, but his poor ears had been battered by all the noise.

'Everyone, look here,' Faizan called out to his class and everyone shouted in response. Some showed mild irritation at being interrupted, while some looked interested. He picked up a creepy cake with a skeleton frosted on it and smashed it onto a seventh grader's face.

'No!' Jimmy protested, 'you've ruined my face paint!'

Sameer knew he had promised himself that he would go back soon, but he was too entertained. So much so that he had totally forgotten that he had only come to check if that bang had caused any serious harm. Sameer caught sight of Ravi in the crowd and approached him. As soon as Ravi saw Sameer, he grabbed his hand and led him to a stall decorated with paper skeletons.

'Wait, I just saw this stall offering a chance to show your musical skills... Let me get my guitar from the—' Sameer began, but he was interrupted by Ravi.

'What are you doing here? Are you alright now? And where on earth is your costume?' Ravi almost shrieked in his ears.

Without giving him a chance to speak, he yelled again, 'You didn't hear about "no-costume-no-party", freaking dunce?'

Ravi was clearly embarrassed by his friend turning up in his PJs.

'You look like a clown,' Ravi wasn't done insulting his friend. 'No, not even a clown. *I* look like a clown,' he boasted. 'And, you can get your guitar later; let's go get those temporary tattoos,' he continued, 'Babar just got one, they're crazy cool!' Just as the boys turned a corner to get into the never-ending queue, a collective gasp interspersed with shrieks caught both the boys' attention. They jogged back towards the crowd to see what the commotion was all about.

As the hostel warden, Mr Nadeem, came out of his office, calling off the party as it was 'too noisy', he found all the boys frozen on the spot; shock, disbelief and horror written on everyone's faces.

He followed their gaze to see that someone wearing a mask lay sprawled on the floor. He immediately bent down to check and the expression on his face confirmed what they already suspected.

It was a dead body.

NINE

'Out everyone, now! Back to your dorms!' Mr Nadeem's hoarse yell dispersed the crowds pretty quickly.

An announcement was made to evacuate the students from the compound. And to make sure no student was stupid enough to go snooping around, he made another announcement later, 'If anyone dares to stay on the playground as I speak, he shall be permanently expelled from the school.'

The ground was empty within a minute of the announcement. Sameer was not in the common room to join in on the gossip with his classmates—he kept to himself. Half an hour later, the head boy packed off everyone to their rooms and strictly told them to stay there until further orders.

Sameer was in his room, thinking about the horrific occurrence of the evening. There had been nothing strange about the night leading to the accident, other than the bang he had heard down the dorms. His mind was in a whirl. Sameer hadn't been at the party since its beginning. The other important thing to remember was that everyone attending the party was in costume and their faces were covered with masks. Sameer also reminded himself that there was no apparent sign of a wound on the body.

Sameer was suddenly scared of being alone in his tiny dormitory. He had thought of the private room as a privilege, but despite the cardboard-thin walls of the room, he could hear nothing. He felt the silence engulfing the entire hostel like the huge cloak of a wizard.

That night, Sameer had nothing to complain about. There was no noise, no shouting. He could not think of putting on his earphones because he feared that someone might silently creep up on him and leave him as lifeless as the dead body on the campus ground.

Sameer suddenly heard the screeching of cars. He jumped out of his bed and pulling up the blinds, looked below to see the large expanse of the ground. The headmaster, the administrator and the members of the management all walked hurriedly, with flabbergasted expressions on their faces. They disappeared into the building. Sameer could not see them anymore. He could only imagine the faces of those people when they would see the dead boy. Still, Sameer wildly hoped that the body was not real, but actually a dummy.

As he moved away from the window, he was creeped out by his own reflection in the mirror — white, as if the blood had drained out of his face. He looked like a dead body himself.

The morning classes of the day had been cancelled yet again. It was their second day of being locked up. It was, after all, an actual body and the only reason they were being kept inside their rooms was so that the investigation could be carried out. The day-students had been given two consecutive days off, and since most of them hadn't experienced the privilege of attending the hostel graduate party, they hadn't witnessed the crime scene. The clerks in the administration office had sent text messages to the parents to not bring the boys to school due to an 'extraordinary situation'. However, the boarders had to be kept inside their dorms. The warden had been taking rounds of all four wings, randomly tapping at the doors of the room and peeping inside, watchful as a hawk.

Although the boys had had nothing to do inside their rooms other than study or sleep, Sameer was one fidgety boy who was not capable of either of the two activities at that time. He had opened the chapter on climate in the Geography book and had gone through it twice over, but realized that he was only reading the words and looking at the maps again and again without actually processing anything. This way, he was not going to be prepared for the test anyway. He knew that the very strict Ms Nadia could be very mean to him for the rest of the term if he didn't score well in the upcoming mock exam. But Sameer's brain refused to comply and he had to give up. He slammed his books shut and looked at his hand, which was shaking with nervousness.

He had been beating himself up for not attending the party earlier. Maybe he could have seen something. Sameer, the anti-social boy who chose to stay aloof, had a flip side to his personality. He was an observer. He observed the atmosphere around him, the behaviour of the people and their actions. He learnt a lot this way and tailored his actions based on the facts he had gathered. He was confident that if he had been around during the celebration that night, he could have found some clue.

He got up from the chair he had been sitting on for the past several hours, and looked at his wristwatch. It was still an hour before lunchtime. He was looking forward to the lunch break, since that had been his only chance to see Ravi in the past few days. They would share with each other everything they had noticed about the strange event. Sameer lay down with his eyes closed and tried to recall the happenings of the past week. As the memories started flooding him, he jumped up, dashed towards the study table and started noting down the events of the past three days as they had happened.

Day 1: The Party

The students had been told by the school authorities to report back to their dorms as soon as possible so that they could be counted among the safe and secure. The pupils who had spotted the body earlier must have had a better chance at figuring out whether it was a homicide or an accident.

Day 2: The Silence

All classes had been called off. The boys were locked in their dormitories with guards outside every five doors. I was devastated upon learning that we couldn't visit each others' dorms, even under supervision. The administration had probably thought that discussions would lead to unnecessary gossip and rumours.

While otherwise the pupils would have thought of it to be a lucky day, they knew exactly why they weren't allowed out. It was quite hard for me as I stayed alone. My head was whirling with myriad thoughts, but I had no one to share them with. Everyone must be silently wondering why the police hadn't come and questioned them yet. They must also be afraid of speaking too soon.

Days 3 and 4: The Curiosity

I was trying to solve the case on my own, which was the only option now. It was a huge risk. I had drawn a sketch of the body and was now trying to remember the physical features of my school fellows to try and match it with the body's. I drew the victim's elbow and part of the jawline that was visible, despite the mask. I was extremely infuriated, unable to find a match. I even went as far as searching the library for the students' pictures in the yearly school magazine. I assume that the victim was one of the graduates.

Unable to find any matches in the yearbook, I threw my hands in the air in exasperation. I anxiously tapped my notepad with the pen, while biting one of my fingernails. I sighed, disappointedly closed the yearbook and gathered my stuff. I put the yearbook under my notepad and purposely left my pen on one of the shelves as it had run out of ink. The librarian's snores could be heard, but I didn't want to take any further risks, and therefore made the poor decision of sitting back down behind one of the heavily stocked shelves, with my legs crossed. I hopelessly opened the yearbook back again, wishing for an angel to come and change its content.

I'd decided to spend the rest of the day in the library. I had to play hide-and-seek in order to stay away from the guards' vision when they took rounds of the room. I hadn't thought of that!

The next morning, I'd woken with a terrible headache and shoulder pain. I had fallen asleep in the library! Not having my watch (I wonder why) to keep track of time worsened my anxiety. I swiftly but silently got up and rushed to open the door, only to almost run into the library teacher. However, I was relieved to see that even past dawn, the teacher was sleepwalking with her eye mask on. Keeping quiet was the only way to get out now.

Though she was one of my least favourite teachers, I was afraid that she might get hurt. But I was in a hurry and rushed out of the room as soon as she was out of my way. I felt guilty – just a bit – but Ravi needed to be found immediately. I wanted to know exactly who the victim was and fortunately, Ravi always kept himself updated on gossip.

Just a step away from my dorm, I thought I'd made it out safely, when the guards (finally) caught me! They sure knew their job. I knew it was going to be a bad day when they greeted me with an annoyed 'Where have you been?' I now knew that I had lost all my chances of communicating with Ravi when they began to drag me towards the headmaster's office. For the sake of solving a murder, I even offered the guards my oh-so-precious hazelnut-filled chocolates as compensation. They were not accepted, which, really, was an insult to those chocolates – but anyway. At least I tried. Now was the time I wished that I had never thought of going to the library, as the results proved to be completely useless.

Once at the headmaster's office, I knew I was in serious trouble. I was definitely scared of being questioned and knew it would sound really silly to say, 'I tried to be a clever fox and solve the murder on my own, but miserably failed'. I had to say something though. I, being myself, spoke my thoughts out loud after, of course, filtering the few necessary-but-not-really adjectives.

Just then, another boy entered the room. He just so happened to be Ravi, who, like me, had likely been looking for clues. In his case, Ravi actually succeeded. We both were thoroughly lectured and wrongly accused for trying to communicate with each other since the past few days. What the headmaster didn't realize was that we both had similar instincts, set on solving the murder. Moreover, he probably thought we had been involved in the 'incident', being the only ones to have defied the school rules then (and in my case, even at the party!).

We'd gotten an hour-long detention inside the office that made us curse the school management. We both had missed lunch break; therefore, we had no information whatsoever on new suspects.

Though we were determined on asking a similar question, neither of us really had the guts to straight up ask the headmaster for possible suspects and victims. We felt defeated and hadn't spoken a word since the headmaster had left his office to check on new updates.

Ravi looked as if he couldn't control himself and spit out the word that left me even more perplexed than I already was.

'Adnan.'

I was about to ask whether he was a suspect or the victim but, um, hard luck. At that very moment, the headmaster stormed in, particularly upset about something and took his frustration out on poor Ravi and me.

'Silence!' he roared, though the only thing I could focus on at the moment was the need to tally my sketches with Adnan's photos.

Sameer remembered how he had been taken back to his dorm after an hour, just the way he was brought in. He preferred not to write that part down; it was already pretty obvious. He also remembered how, just a few hours ago, Ravi mentioned Adnan. After much head-scratching, Sameer remembered who Adnan was. He wasn't a very well-known boy, and Ravi was right, perhaps involving himself in the incident was a move to gain popularity. He might also remain unsuspected as the unpopular guys are hardly ever questioned properly.

'But I didn't see him at lunch break yesterday...' Sameer's voice trailed off. He suddenly had a moment of realization—'The body is his! Adnan is the victim here!'

It was a moment of victory, but also one that frightened him. There were still ten minutes till lunch break and Sameer couldn't wait to share his thoughts on the possible victims and suspects with Ravi. Perhaps, for the first time ever, he would even take someone else's opinion, because he wasn't certain about anything.

Soon it was lunch time, and the students took their places on their table. It could have looked like business as usual, however, this time, the police surrounded them. Ravi and Sameer both spotted each other in the crowd and both started walking towards one another.

'They haven't left yet?' Sameer started the conversation.

'Apparently not.' Ravi was sadder than Sameer had ever seen him.

'So you mean to say, the police has just been chilling around at Kingston High for the past few days?'

'Uh, apparently.'

'Hey, what's up with you, no witty remarks today?'

Sameer had been silent for most part during this whole ruckus, while simultaneously tugging at Ravi's sleeve to get his attention. Ravi got irritated and stood up, loudly clearing his throat, and catching half of the students' attention, which was enough.

Ravi had correctly assumed what Sameer was bothering him about and began, 'My friend here,' Ravi paused to look at Sameer, 'has a question.'

Sameer, who wasn't good with crowds, glared at his friend for a good few seconds. The boys stared at him and he had no choice but to stare back with a clueless expression. Ravi shook his head with a disappointed 'You'll never learn' look and asked the question himself. 'Possible murder victims and suspects. Tell me right now.' Ravi spoke in the most demanding tone he could muster. Sameer knew no one would respond and probably think that he and his friend were mad. But he was proven wrong when people actually came up with names, though they were only guesses, with no actual proof.

TEN

'Adnan!'
This name was chanted by most of the boys, one after the other. Adnan was nowhere to be seen those days, obviously making him the number one suspect or victim. This theory had potential and could be easily accepted by the police. Sameer wondered when the police would actually question them.

'Asim!'

The second most popular name was yelled by several students. This guess was very random and didn't have potential, unlike the first one, but was a good possibility, as Asim was the only worker at the school who befriended the students. And Sameer knew a few secrets about Asim that could help in proving him to be the murderer.

The renowned 'psychic' of the school, a rather awkward boy, Navid, meekly muttered, 'The boy you feuded with,' he paused, as if in deep thought, 'his friend.'

'Huh, the captain of the football team?' Ravi whispered to Sameer.

'Faizan?'

'Yeah, you replaced his best friend as the co-captain, remember?'

Sameer had barely had a full conversation when he was rudely interrupted.

'Silence!' A rowdy voice roared. It was a police officer. Though the whole school had quietened at the last prediction, the officers had to find a way to get the boys' attention. They were unaware of how curious the boys already were.

'We're here to inform you boys about the body, so incorrect assumptions can stop.'

'Oh, and you, especially, stop spreading rumours,' the same officer stated, emphasizing on the word 'stop'. Sameer cringed when he realized that the words were directed at him.

Sameer wasn't making assumptions, he thought to himself, annoyed with the officers. He was only trying to put two and two together based on others' assumptions. Just before he turned his focus back to the officers, from the corner of his eye, he caught a glimpse of Faizan.

He was indeed alive, and well.

'The incident did turn out to be a homicide. And no further discussion on this topic between the pupils, would definitely be appreciated,' the officer said in a gruff voice. He continued, 'Our top murder suspect is one of you sitting right there on table number...' He paused briefly before saying, 'Four.'

This caused all the boys to instantly turn to table four. Only three people were sitting there—Navid, the psychic, paid no attention to this news, with his head bent over his plate of food; Faizan, also on the same table, only raised an eyebrow and scoffed; and Sir Aslam, who sat opposite the two boys, began nervously tugging at his beard.

∽

Instead of quieting down, the boys gossiped their way throughout lunch.

Sameer didn't know how to react and decided he shouldn't, considering nothing had been confirmed yet.

'Foolish kids,' he muttered, sighing. If he were part of the law enforcement and had to give out information, it would have definitely been solid. He chuckled in disappointment when he thought how the officer had distracted them enough to forget about the biggest question mark—who the victim was.

Sameer hadn't noticed in his reverie that the police had left the hall, leaving the students to talk among themselves. It was a good time to analyse the information.

Adnan was an obvious potential victim as he hadn't been seen for days, according to his friends. Asim was very popular among the boys as he had befriended most of them. Thus, there was no reason for him to harm anybody—Sameer thought he had been genuine in his friendship with him and Ravi. Sameer hoped that Asim was out of trouble. Of course, the boys were being served their meals thrice a day, so Asim still had dishes to wash. Sameer wished most sincerely that his friend was no more sneaking around and was just sticking to his business. He finally snapped out of his thoughts.

'We need to come up with a plan,' Sameer said to his friend, 'and quick. We need to get the officers to reveal who the body belonged to, collect evidence and reveal the murderer, and most importantly, see for ourselves if any body even exists, if someone was even murdered.'

Ravi looked at his friend, wide-eyed and astonished by his wild thoughts. It wasn't that Sameer's ideas were not worthwhile. But it seemed to Ravi that it would be completely ridiculous to question the existence of the dead body, which more than half of the school had witnessed.

Both boys had now silently started thinking of plans. However, Sameer's mind kept wandering back to the same thought: How had no one witnessed the victim actually dying? It was as if the body fell out of nowhere.

Sameer definitely knew it was an audacious thought, but he dared to think that it wasn't a murder after all. Maybe it was a suicide. A murder would definitely have caused a mess. A conflict would have happened if it actually were a murder, and Sameer wasn't aware of any conflict between the boys.

There was another option—if there weren't any serious feuds amongst the boys, someone could have accidently harmed the other. Shaking all thoughts out of his head, Sameer remembered that this was his only time of freedom. Later, he would have all the time in the world, trapped in his dorm, to think.

He advised the same to Ravi, worried that he would be the one to cause his friend brain damage from overthinking.

It seemed as if all the pupils in the hall were living in different worlds. On table number four, Navid, Faizan and Sir Aslam had started pointed fingers at each other.

'Well, I was busy smashing cake on people's faces! Ask Jimmy.'

'Hmm, I still have a feeling it was you, *captain.*'

Faizan ignored the psychic boy, while Sir Aslam intervened, 'Stop it, you two!'

'Was it you then?' Faizan questioned, making poor Sir Aslam tug at his beard once again.

The boys sitting at the main sixteen-seater table were laughing and eating. Some nerds ate in an awkward silence. Sameer's table would eat in silence for one minute, but the other, they would be sharing their ideas about the suspects and victims.

This continued for another fifteen minutes until Faizan shouted anxiously 'Where on earth is Rauf?'

The boys took a while to process Faizan's words

and when they did, their horror-struck faces seemed frozen in place. Most of the students claimed that Rauf was the victim, while others assumed that he was the murderer. Sameer stuck with the former, as he knew the steps followed by a successful murderer: Kill. Remove evidence. Blend in.

And if this was his attempt at blending in, Rauf had miserably failed. Sameer was sure that Rauf wasn't stupid. He cut off Rauf from his list of murderers and underlined the name in red in his victim list.

The lunch hour finished sooner than expected, and despite knowing that they had to return to their respective dorms, the boys were obviously too curious to abide by the rules in such an exceptional situation. They had gotten together—some in pairs, and some in larger groups—and were proceeding towards their rooms.

Sameer and Ravi had ended up in Faizan's dorm, along with a few of the other players on the football team. It was chaotic and the boys were out of control. The security guards had given up, while the halls became more and more crowded. Many had lined outside the dorms of 'popular kids', and doors were invitingly kept open.

The boys had had enough of being locked up in their lonely dorms. The least they could do was make use of available company, and together solve the murder case of a fellow student.

The conversation had started with Faizan shoving Sameer into the wall. Sameer immediately regretted his decision of sticking with Ravi, just as Ravi regretted bringing Sameer along.

'I didn't think you had the guts,' Faizan said softly, shaking his head, 'Clearly I was wrong!'

At this point, Sameer had been shoved into the wall twice, in front of a few other people including his best friend, and he wasn't going to take it anymore. He pushed back.

'Listen here,' Sameer retorted angrily, 'I'm not going to stand here and ask you what you're talking about, because I am aware of just how stupid you are!'

He calmed down and slowly said the words, 'I did not kill your friend.' In return, he got some 'I don't believe you' and some 'I know right' looks. After he was sure he had made his point, Sameer stomped towards the door and yanked it open. Ravi followed close behind, but upon reaching his dorm, he wasted no time in slamming the door shut, not even allowing his friend in.

Sameer was boiling with anger, furious at his friend and of course, at Faizan. He couldn't believe that even other pupils thought of him as the culprit. His eyes scanned the place that he could hardly call a room, and looked for something to calm his frayed nerves. He glanced at his iPod and decided to listen to his favourite grunge rock playlist, but instead of calming him, he felt the sudden urge to throw it at someone's head, particularly Ravi's. If he had not gone into Faizan's room, that fight would've probably not happened.

Faizan's misconception had gone too far and while he knew that Rauf was his best friend and Sameer would have done the same if anything happened to Ravi, he would have thought sensibly before making unforgivably horrible assumptions.

Sameer soon realized it was a good thing that he followed his friend, despite the humiliation. At least he knew what he was going to be dealing with.

Eventually, Sameer calmed down after penning his thoughts in his dear diary. He settled down and opened his Chemistry books. Though he was feeling bored all alone in his dorm, he still wasn't in any mood to greet his friend with open arms.

Just as he had found something to do, Sameer jumped in his seat, startled at the unexpected ringing of the bell. It was not the usual bell that indicated the end of a class; this one was for an important discussion to be held in the assembly area. Sameer was intrigued but unsure of whether to go or not.

After taking a peep outside, he joined the rest of the pupils in the now crowded passageway, bumping occasionally into each other as they all walked towards the hall. Sameer hadn't noticed throughout the chaos that Ravi had been alongside him. Fidgety and anxious, he worried that the announcement might bring some very bad news...

The boys had settled in rows within seconds, as they had been taught the importance of discipline from day one at the school.

Glancing at the police, who were standing some distance away, Sameer knew that this announcement would actually be informative and not just something cryptic to mess with the students.

Sameer glanced around to make sure that the younger students hadn't snuck in, as they were forbidden to do so. It was a really difficult situation for the older students themselves; he could only imagine what must've gone through the younger ones' minds upon hearing about a murder. At least they were not involved in the investigation itself; the sight of the police would scare the living daylights out of them.

This time, instead of the headmaster addressing them, the microphone was confidently handed over to the officer.

'Good morning.'

The fairly well-mannered children, including Sameer, replied in unison, 'Good morning to you too.'

'As you all know, an extraordinary situation has taken place in the school, for which school rules have been intensely modified. But we brought you all out here to finally reveal the name of the victim, and put you all to ease. Hopefully.'

The microphone was then handed over to Officer Salman. Sameer figured that he was at the head of the investigation, considering he was the only one to wear a badge. Sameer couldn't help but notice that he stood upright with a little bit of arrogance.

There was one long minute's silence before the officer spoke another word. That minute was a torture for all the boys. Sameer was sure that by now, everyone was aware of the 'Rauf situation'. Still, the police had proof of the body, and any confirmation would be a great stress reliever and reassurance for the boys.

To create a dramatic effect and to make his revelation more effective, Officer Salman sighed deeply before continuing. Sameer was surprised at the headmaster's neutral expression throughout these histrionics. Meanwhile, the boys, some anxious and some annoyed, waited for the revelation. Some extremely scared students looked as if their eyes were about to burst out of their sockets, in anticipation of the news to follow.

'The body belongs to Rauf Nawaz.'

Despite the boys being aware of the already popular theory, they were stunned and couldn't quite get themselves to believe the statement.

Sameer, at that point, knew that it didn't matter as much to Faizan that his best friend was dead. It didn't matter to the other boys that one of their best football players had died. What really mattered to them was the fact such an unfortunate incident had occurred at

Kingston High! Sameer couldn't believe that a horrific occurrence could take place at a heavily guarded school like his.

After a good two minutes, when the boys had finally recovered from the shock, Sameer and Ravi looked at each other. Even though Ravi had been the rowdy, tough type of guy, this time, he seemed to have become the scaredy cat. Sameer felt bad for him and the rest of the boys, but also for himself. This was his first year being at the new school, and it seemed as if it was going to be spent solving a murder.

In a matter of minutes, the dead silence of the auditorium turned into an unexplainable, unbelievably loud commotion. The boys completely forgot about the presence of the police; and while they could have been punished for being disrespectful, the police and the headmaster were aware of the extraordinary situation, and let the boys vent their feelings.

Sameer was involved in a group discussion, where he listened to people's rants, complaints and grief. Some of the students had even started sobbing and showed no signs of stopping anytime soon. Sameer had noticed Ravi leave, but didn't bother asking after him. It wasn't because of any grudge that he held against him, but because he knew that Ravi had gone to look for more clues.

Meanwhile, Sameer multitasked — he listened to the students and analysed the information, but he also kept one eye on the police team to figure out what they were arguing about amongst themselves.

He was attentively following the police's expressions, and saw that Officer Salman had come to a decision. He murmured a few words to the headmaster and straightened up, while the headmaster clapped his hands to bring the attention of the boys back to the police.

'We have another announcement to make…' Officer Salman's face looked almost pitiful. Almost.

'The body has just recently gone…missing.'

He said the next sentence with a vicious smirk that showed that he had no pity left in him, 'And don't worry, we shall all find the body together and for that, each and every single one of you are about to be thoroughly questioned.'

ELEVEN

The boys, rather than claiming to have had nothing to do with the situation, jumped around foolishly with anticipation. They thought they would be filled in on all the information the police had gathered. Sameer and Ravi were rather excited.

A team of officers was brought in, with one officer assigned to each class, which were assembled in lines. One by one, each student was called into an empty auditorium to be questioned. Finally, after the 'O' and 'A' level students were done, and after a few good hours of exasperation, the eighth-grade students finally had their turn. To be honest, Sameer was looking forward to talking to the police, especially since he wanted to help solve the murder.

Sameer would have liked to think that he was walking into the auditorium with total confidence and a determination to reveal something that could help the investigation, but he actually walked in breathing heavily, with sweaty hands. His stress was quite evident.

'Hi, what's your name?' asked the officer.

'Sameer,' he responded briefly.

'Sameer,' the officer paused, 'let's start with you. Did you see Rauf before the incident?'

'Well, actually, the night of the murder, I wasn't at the party at first—'

'Just try to answer the question please.'

'But it's necessary,' Sameer continued, 'I hadn't attended the party in the beginning and wouldn't even have. Then I heard a loud bang, which seemed to come from near the kitchen larder, but I was sure no one paid any attention to it since the boys were all at the party; there was a lot of music and shouting. So, I decided to go check it out for myself. After I reached the very last step of the staircase, I got distracted. Pulled into the crowd. I didn't realize till very late that I hadn't done what I had intended to. At that moment, it also seemed stupid, so I...just dropped it.'

'What are you trying to say, exactly?'

'That maybe, somehow the murder was planned... or set up. Someone was desperate for attention. And that you need to seriously figure out what was going on in the larder.'

The police were obviously not going to listen to an eight grader's suggestion; after all, a larder is a larder and sometimes pots and pans fall on their own. But what the police couldn't quite understand was that it wasn't that simple.

Officer Salman tried his hardest not to laugh out loud at the boy, 'Is that it?' He rephrased his long-forgotten question, 'Which part, or parts, of the homicide did you witness?'

Sameer raised his finger, indicating the first event, 'The bang under my dorm, probably the starting,' Sameer paused, 'and the end result—the dead body.'

'Were you with someone else, or alone, when you saw the body?'

'With my friend, Ravi.'

Sameer's reply made the officer check the 'R' list of pupils.

The officer raised his brows before asking the last question, 'Did you think that one of your fellow pupils seemed suspicious?'

'No one in particular. I don't think so.'

'Okay, boy. Get out.' With these words of the officer, Sameer realized it was his best friend's turn next. He would definitely be far nosier than Sameer, not that he considered that a problem. Officer Salman surely deserved to be annoyed, and Ravi would do quite an excellent job at that.

Sameer went out of the office and stood with those who had already been interrogated. From a distance, he could hear the officer calling out Ravi's name. He looked at the crowd of students.

'Where is he?' Sameer thought out aloud, when someone nudged his shoulder. He jumped.

'How is it in there?' Ravi, being the easy-going person he was, was apparently taking it all very coolly.

'Ugh, go see for yourself!' Sameer snapped.

Ravi shrugged and went in for his moment of grilling.

The boys were not allowed to leave the premises until ordered. So, Sameer grabbed the only copy of a news magazine lying on the book rack and started reading about the new robot waitress strolling around in the restaurants of Japan and cutting the workload of humans.

'Duh.' Sameer flipped the pages, found nothing else interesting and slumped against the wall, thinking about the chemical reactions that could be done with sodium hydroxide and quadinium carbonate.

As the boys chatted and played little games as they patiently sat through the investigations, the auditorium suddenly boomed with the high-pitched nasal voice of the headmaster's secretary, Ms Fozia, 'Sameer Abbas, please report immediately to the headmaster's office.'

This was a little confusing, and Sameer thought it was probably a mistake until his name was called out a few more times. After the fifth time, he finally decided to step away from the crowd so he was visible to the other boys who were craning their necks to get a proper view of him.

This is ridiculous, he thought to himself as the boys whispered to each other.

'New boy,' he could hear them say.

'Are you serious?' he asked them all mentally. He had been there for months, and once the suspicion came his way, he had become the 'new boy' again?

'Jokers!' he said softly, and exited the auditorium to go to the headmaster's office.

Sameer sped up a little upon reaching the doors of the office, jogging his way up to the headmaster's desk. He wasn't bothered by the fact that he had been called to the office, even if for all the wrong reasons. This way, at least he could talk to someone who would believe him. He knocked at the door, and Ms Fozia asked him to come in.

'Did you ask for me, Ms Fozia?' Sameer asked meekly.

She wore the same stern expression that had been plastered on her face for the past few days.

'Sit,' she commanded briefly as she picked up her phone and whispered something into it.

Sameer was confused. He had done nothing wrong, but everyone was acting weird with him. He was reminded of the stares and remarks he was getting from the boys of his class.

'New boy,' he muttered with disgust.

'The headmaster will see you now,' Ms Fozia told him and he jumped in his chair, startled to hear her voice cutting through his angry thoughts.

'Thank you,' he said, walking through the door that led him to a very quiet room. The huge desk in front of him was intimidating, but Sameer gathered his guts to look up and see the very sober face of the headmaster.

'Good afternoon, Sir,' Sameer had not forgotten his manners, despite the churning in his stomach.

'Afternoon, Sameer,' the headmaster replied. 'Please meet the police officer who is here with us.'

Sameer looked to his side and saw a tall and handsome man in a casual T-shirt and a pair of jeans on a sofa.

'Good afternoon, S-sir,' Sameer said, stammering a little.

'Good afternoon to you too, Sameer.' The officer seemed friendlier than the ones he had already spoken to.

The headmaster walked from his desk to join the officer on the sofa and asked Sameer to sit with them too. Sameer obeyed.

'Hi, Sameer, I am Officer Bilal. I hear you have already spoken to my colleagues in the auditorium,' he said.

'Just like everyone else,' Sameer was quick to respond.

The officer chuckled, 'Of course.'

'Sameer, reply briefly,' the headmaster hinted with a word of caution.

'Uh yes, Sir,' Sameer replied.

'What were you doing at the larder the afternoon of the party?'

'I...I was playing my guitar.'

'In the larder?'

'Well, because I am not allowed to play guitar in the dorm.'

'Where is the guitar now?'

'Uh...it must be in the larder,' Sameer's voice shook, as he felt he was being suspected.

'When did you last play?'

'That afternoon, before the party, because we haven't been let out of the dorm since then.' Sameer was getting flustered.

'Oh, but the headmaster here tells me that you managed to sneak out of your dorm once, despite being grounded,' the inspector said calmly.

'I went...to get the yearbook and see...my friend. But I was caught! Midway!'

'Yes, I heard. That doesn't matter. You had the guts to rebel. That is my first crumb, Sameer,' Inspector Bilal stared very deeply into his eyes and Sameer shuddered.

'Is this true that you replaced Rauf as the co-captain of the football team and you two were not very friendly for the past few months?'

'What? No. I mean, yes, I replaced him, but we were cool. Who said otherwise?' said Sameer, his voice steadily ascending in pitch.

'There is no need to get loud, Sameer,' the headmaster gave a warning look.

'That would be all, Sameer.' Inspector Bilal had a

very smug look on his face as he stood up.

'You can go now,' the headmaster signalled to Sameer and he left the room. He was feeling flustered, agitated and annoyed. As he entered Ms Fozia's room, he saw the lab assistant from the senior science laboratory. He was looking very worried and as Sameer walked through the room, Ms Fozia looked at him over the rim of her reading glasses. She saw that he looked pale and immediately stood up with concern, asking him to sit down.

'Are you all right?' she asked as she offered him a glass of water.

'I guess,' he said. She made him sit on a chair, while the lab assistant looked extremely offended with the disturbance Sameer had caused.

'Ms Fozia,' the assistant said through gritted teeth. 'This is an absolutely important and urgent issue,' he almost hissed.

'I know, I can understand,' she replied coolly.

'Ms Fozia, the sudden disappearance of quadinium carbonate and sodium hydroxide is not a simple case of theft; it is a very dangerous theft with very grave consequences,' the assistant insisted.

'I said I understand, and I hope you also understand we do not discuss certain issues in front of the students.'

The assistant did not reply.

'Also, before you trouble the headmaster with this issue, I suggest you go back and try harder to look for the stolen or misplaced chemicals since they were your responsibility.' Ms Fozia could be very scary when she wanted to be.

The lab assistant excused himself from the room and Sameer, having recovered from the meeting and feeling less shaky, was allowed to leave for his dorm. Outside his hostel, he saw some boys looking suspiciously at him, but he pretended to ignore their stares. He felt like someone had stabbed him in the heart.

Outside the dorm, he found Ravi waiting anxiously for him.

'Hey, all well? What happened?' he asked Sameer.

'Why? You aren't going to whisper and gossip about the "new boy"?'

'Come on, buddy, you know how things get out of hand here pretty quick. Don't worry!'

'I need to be alone, Ravi,' Sameer said in the quietest voice.

'All right,' Ravi, for once, understood that Sameer had had a rough day. He did not try to cheer him up, but gave him the privacy he needed. Sameer looked at his dear iPod, the tablet, the magazine and the keys to his gym locker. Nothing interested him. He shut his eyes to give them some relief. Twisting and turning in his bed brought no peace to his throbbing brain, for it kept replaying every bit of the conversations he had been and not been part of, throughout the day. Eventually, he fell into an uneasy sleep.

Around midnight, when he was very close to the threshold of sleep, he suddenly sat up in his bed, eyes wide open, gaping, breathless, like he had seen a ghost!

TWELVE

The headmaster's room was cool, since the ceiling was pretty high. The arched windows were tightly shut, the blinds closed and the door locked with Ms Fozia standing guard like a hawk. The four boys, Sameer, Faizan, Asim — and Rauf — stood in a line in front of the headmaster's desk. He and Inspector Bilal sat across the desk and stared hard at the boys. There was an amused look on Inspector Bilal's face, but a cold, steely expression on the headmaster's.

'Can you tell us once again, Sameer, what occurred to you?'

'Erm...about Rauf being the dead body or the chemical thing?'

'Both, please, but start with the chemical reaction.'

'Uh...okay. Well, the other day, I heard the lab assistant from the senior Chemistry lab tell Ms Fozia about the sudden theft of two chemicals, quadinium carbonate and sodium hydroxide, from the laboratory. He said it happened just a day before the party.'

'Why did you not tell Ms Fozia about your eureka moment at that time?' Inspector Bilal asked.

'I...didn't realize it at that time. It just occurred to

me near midnight.'

'Alright. Please carry on.'

'I told this to Ms Fozia immediately. She is the warden of the hostel's North Wing. I felt I had to tell someone urgently.'

'You did a smart thing, Sameer,' the headmaster spoke for the first time. His voice was as cold as ice.

'I did not know where Rauf could have hidden all this time, but Ms Fozia took me to the laboratory immediately and looked at the register in which every student has to sign when they use the lab.'

'And what did you find there?'

'We saw the names of Rauf and Faizan on the day of the party.'

'What exactly do these two chemicals do, Sameer?' Inspector Bilal's question was directed at him, but he was looking at Rauf and Faizan.

'It can slow down the heartbeat for a few minutes and put the person who takes it, to a deep sleep. The deep sleep reduces the level of oxygen in the lungs and the bloodstream, so the face can go pale and the body temperature can drop. These could have been the signs that led the headmaster and warden to believe they were touching a dead body. Since no one except them touched the body at that time, only they can confirm my scientific observations.'

'Interesting.' Inspector Bilal had gotten up from his seat and was walking towards the boys. 'Doesn't it harm the body when it stays inside the system?' The inspector's question was directed at Ms Fozia, who gulped nervously before she answered, 'It passes out with urine.'

The inspector nodded thoughtfully.

'One word for you, Rauf and Faizan—WHY?' he asked.

'I am sorry, I am truly very sorry. I only meant it as a prank,' Faizan was the first one to talk and he really seemed upset and ashamed.

'Did you two steal the chemicals and prepare the concoction?' The headmaster was not interested in Faizan's tears.

'Yes, Sir,' Faizan said very softly.

'WHY?' the headmaster thundered.

'For the prank, Sir. I just meant it for the prank. I...we...Rauf and I wanted to win the Mr Genius title so badly, we were just doing a prank and we wanted Sameer to lose. We know how good he is with the ball on the field and the experiments in the laboratory. Rauf told me it would just be for a few hours but then, when he disappeared, even I didn't know where he had gone, or how, so I didn't say a word. He was my friend and I got overprotective and thought that this was Sameer's idea of a prank. Murdering my best friend.'

He looked over at Sameer, 'I am truly sorry.'

Sameer couldn't bring himself to respond.

'Do you know you could be expelled?' the headmaster asked Faizan, who just shook his head.

'Where have you been hiding, Rauf?'

'You found me, Sir, you know where,' Rauf was stubborn as an ox.

'We need to hear from you, again.'

'I was in the larder. The abandoned one, right under Sameer's bedroom,' Rauf said.

'How come we didn't find you there when we checked the building?'

'Well, because I am smarter than all of you, and also because you people did not check the floorboards. Four of the floorboards are creaky, and they open into a small war-shelter.'

'Headmaster, was this war-shelter to your knowledge?'

'I have looked up the original plan of the school and yes, since it was built in the 1800s, this school—like every other—had a small war-shelter. I never thought it could be discovered.'

'I found it two years ago! It was my hideout, my own little place until this clown came in to play guitar in that room of mine!' Rauf pointed at Sameer.

Sameer's ears reddened with anger.

'Behave, Rauf!' the headmaster thundered again.

'You have been given a dorm, Rauf. That is your room. Neither you nor Sameer is allowed to go to the larder, but that boy can be excused for being a hero.

You, on the other hand, have been a troublemaker and cannot be spared.'

'Hero? Seriously?' Rauf exclaimed and gave Sameer a dirty look.

'Yes, a hero. He figured out your conduct, took us into confidence and led us to Asim, your accomplice.'

Asim shook with fear.

'So, Asim, why did you not help the police?' Inspector Bilal asked his last question to Asim.

'I was afraid. I was just afraid. Rauf told me he will come out in a day or two, but he made it too long. I brought him food from the kitchen, because I worried he might die...for real. I begged him each time to come out, but he wouldn't. I am sorry, I really am.'

'Well, I am thankful to you Sameer, for leading us to Asim. If you hadn't told us about Asim boasting of knowing a secret place within the school premises, among other secrets, we would never have gotten it out of him.' Inspector Bilal shook Sameer's hand like a friend, patted his shoulder and asked him to leave. 'Attend to your studies. These foolish boys have already cost you all a week.'

Sameer could not leave without putting in a good word for Asim. 'Sir, I have a request. Asim is not a bad guy. He may bend the rules sometimes, but he was just trying to be friendly. He has a good heart.'

He knew Asim more than any of them did. He remembered the day when Asim took him and Ravi to his school. He had probably done it before with other boys as well, in an attempt to prove he was no less than them, just because he worked in the kitchen at their school.

'We appreciate your concern for Asim. We have to maintain strict discipline and he has involved himself in some serious misadventure. We shall do what is just, to both Rauf and to Asim. You should be at ease now, and go to your dorm,' the headmaster replied.

Sameer obeyed the order and walked out like a hero. He also received a rare smile from Ms Fozia.

Once out, he closed his eyes and smiled, breathing deeply. The air seemed lighter and the sun seemed brighter. He jumped out of his skin when someone slapped his back in that moment of quiet.

It was Ravi!

'Hey, what happened? You found him? Where? How? He is alive? That super jerk! I want details, all of them. Now. NOW!' Ravi was excitedly jumping around a laughing Sameer. Some other boys also gathered around them excitedly, jumping and laughing just like boys of fourteen should.

THIRTEEN

Fall and winter had gone by in quick succession. Both the school trip and the party that had led to such a huge controversy had turned out to be the biggest highlights of that year, not only for the eighth graders but for the entire school. The boarders had been ordered to not share a word with the other students and so, the secret was being guarded by every single student of the school, right from the primary classes to older ones!

'That's been some year!' Ravi said to Sameer as they both sat on the steps outside the school auditorium. They were both sharing a paper cone filled with salted popcorn.

'Yeah,' Sameer said, smiling. He still had the small badge of honour given to him and Ravi by the management of the Lahore Heritage Museum for helping to make a very valuable addition to the collection at their museum. Ravi had packed his away as he was paranoid about losing or damaging it. He hadn't even peeled the plastic covering off the case that held the badge.

'I will show it to my mother and father first. Open it with them,' Ravi said. Though he fooled around all the time, he used to get emotional while remembering his parents.

'Remember the fright we got inside that cleft in the wall?' Sameer said, right out of the blue.

'Hahaha, oh yes. It was like getting inside some enchanted cave, yeah?'

Ravi and Sameer laughed at the memories.

'You ever think about what might have happened to Asim?'

'You mean you don't know?' Ravi was surprised.

'No, what do I not know?' It was Sameer's turn to be surprised.

'He was given a stipend in place of the job in the school.'

'Well, that is good,' Sameer said, a little sad at losing a friend he had rather liked.

'I would like to see him at least once more though,' Ravi said longingly.

Both stared ahead for one minute before jerking their heads towards one another.

'Are you thinking what I am thinking?' Sameer asked Ravi, with his eyes twinkling and a mischievous smile on his face, which Ravi knew very well.

'Oh no, no, no, no. I am definitely not thinking that, and shame on you for thinking like that!'

'Oh come on! It won't hurt!'

'I am not getting into another mess with you, thank you very much,' Ravi said, putting his hands up.

'Listen, it's all right, no one will bother today, everyone is packing up. Even the teachers are packing their stuff in the classrooms and staffroom. We can slip out and slip back in easily.'

'Are you kidding? Tell me you are kidding me! You have a PLAN already?'

Sameer shrugged and put on his aviators, pretending to be a hero.

'Show off!' Ravi teased.

'Let's go, Ravi. We need to close this properly. We never got a chance.'

'Yeah. Guy was a good dude.'

'Hahahaha. He is still there. Ravi, let's go see him and say goodbye.'

'I don't know, Sameer, I get jittery about the word "goodbye".'

Sameer stared at his friend for a long time. Ravi looked away, embarrassed.

'You will come back,' Sameer said in an affirmative tone. But he felt nervous. He hadn't thought about goodbyes in that way.

'I guess,' Ravi smiled sadly and stood up. 'So,' he changed his tone immediately, as if trying to change the stressful atmosphere.

'So…' Sameer didn't know whether to force his friend to accompany him on another great misadventure on the last day of the school year.

'Let's go!'

'Seriously?' Sameer was beyond happy.

'Yeah,' Ravi smiled. The boys bumped their fists and ran off.

Faizan saw them on the way out and yelled, 'Hey, what're you both up to now?'

'See you later!' they both yelled back and kept running. The servant's quarter was about two and a half playgrounds away. Once they reached gate number 3, they found that it was open, but the cook, who by now, like the rest of the staff, recognized both of them as the troublemakers-slash-heroes of the school, was standing right in front of it.

'What brings you here, boys?' the cook asked in a gruff voice.

'Umm...' Sameer had lost his voice. This was the first time, a hurdle — a big, bald hurdle — had come between them and a mission.

'We...actually...' Ravi, too, was stammering.

'Well?' the cook's voice became more gruff, and the frown deeper.

'Er, actually we —' Sameer was about to make an honourable speech, when Ravi cut him off.

'Ahem, nothing, we were just checking out the whole school and came to see this part too. And now,' he looked at Sameer, who was caught off guard, 'we are going back to our dorms.'

'We are?' Sameer said, his mouth and eyes both wide open.

'Yes, we indeed are,' Ravi said between gritted teeth.

'Okay,' Sameer didn't push it further.

'Okay. Good. Off with you then!' the cook grunted.

Sameer wanted to give a piece of his mind to Ravi for chickening out. He was only resisting being rude, because Ravi hadn't been too cheerful since the day had started.

'He would have never let us through,' Ravi said softly, understanding his friend's frustration.

'We could have tried,' Sameer replied, without looking at his friend.

'Not with the record we have, not at all,' Ravi tried to reason. Sameer was visibly disappointed. 'We will see him, sometime,' Ravi said, trying to console him as much as he could.

'Yeah,' Sameer said reluctantly. There was no other way. Yet.

The school year had come to an end and it was time for the boarders to go back to their homes. The boys had taken their finals in May and were packing their bags. The exchange programme students had an entirely different process to go through and were to stay at the school for another week. Everyone was hustling.

Ravi had packed his bag a day before. His formal suit, crisp white shirt and red necktie were hanging on a chair in his dorm. He had vacated his own room on the final day and had shifted to Sameer's room, which, in Ravi's opinion, was quite 'unfit'.

'How, my man, do you stack these clothes like my mum?' Ravi was exasperated at the neatly folded clothes. 'It is just not possible!'

Sameer smiled in return and told his friend to get his camera ready so they could click as many photos of the school as they could.

This term had been quieter, peaceful. Rauf had been expelled the same day Inspector Bilal had called Sameer the hero. Faizan had been given a warning, and his parents called up and warned too. But these were privileged boys from rich homes. Asim was the one Sameer felt guilty about. He knew Asim was a rule-bender, but then, so was he. He had lost his job, something he had worked hard at for his family and education. And worse, they never got a chance to say goodbye.

After the curious incident of the 'lost-and-found boy', as the boarders had started calling Rauf, a lot of changes had been made. The headmaster had turned the secret shelter under the larder into a storeroom where the boys could store their personal musical instruments. The floorboards had been ripped up and new, strong tiles were put in their place to cover up any secret basement, so no student could ever get any wild ideas.

Sameer had been happy at the change in the policy to allow students to play in the music room outside the hostel and keep the instruments in the new storeroom. He had, however, nothing to store in there. His guitar was broken mysteriously and Sameer had ignored the desire to investigate who had done it, for he had solved enough mysteries to last the academic year.

'Could be Adnan,' Ravi had thought out loud.

Sameer had just shrugged it off. 'It is done.' He, being a hoarder, had kept the broken guitar in his room, though he had already began thinking about what he wanted for his birthday, which was coming up during the summer holidays.

'You got my email address, don't you?' Sameer checked with Ravi for the millionth time.

'I do,' Ravi smiled back.

Sameer remembered how scared and weird he had felt when he had first come to the school. He was sure for weeks on end that he wouldn't be making any new friends at all and now, at the year end, he was the most talked-about boy at school. He looked at the football trophy in his room, the one given to him as 'Best Player of the Year' during a year-end ceremony for the football team. It made him both happy and sad.

Still, he was looking forward to going home to his dog, Pepper, his sisters, who would tease the living daylights out of him, and also his dear daddy, who had made additions to his Chemistry lab back at home! Most of all, he wanted to be with his mother! He chuckled when he thought of the squeals she would let out, when she would see the trophy and the medal that he received as 'Mr Smart' of the year.

Ravi had received a similar medal, which he wanted to wear on the flight home so that he could surprise his parents as soon as they would see him.

Ravi and Sameer clicked photos at the hostel, the school, the staff room and outside the headmaster's office. The day came to an end and finally, the parking lot started to fill up with the cars of parents who had come to take their boys home.

'So,' Ravi said with a sad smile on his face.

'Write to me,' Sameer was sad too. He didn't feel like smiling.

'Let's always be friends, Sameer,' Ravi held out his hand for Sameer to shake. Sameer extended his arm and hugged his buddy. 'Sure, we both make a good team,' he said with a smile.

'Are you kidding me? We make a fantastic team, dude. We rock!'

'Hahaha, yeah, true.'

'I cannot wait to tell Dad about the scrolls we found at Emperor Jahangir's game reserve. He has been saving the news articles appearing on the Internet since.'

'Hey, you packed your award from the museum, didn't you?'

'Of course!'

'Good...' Sameer was having trouble saying goodbye.

'Hey, isn't your car here already?'

'Must be.'

'Then let's go check your folks out!'

'Yeah,' Sameer grabbed his suitcase and Ravi helped him with the duffel bag. They both walked in the direction of the parking lot when Sameer suddenly froze in his tracks.

'I have an idea!' he almost yelled at Ravi.

'Dear god, I know this look...' Ravi rolled his eyes.

'Listen up, I will tell my parents we have to go see Asim. You understand? And you will come with me definitely!'

'I am supposed to stay back,' Ravi protested.

'I will drop you back at the campus. The parking lot is so crowded; no one will notice you going or coming back.'

The idea was foolproof.

'You want to see Asim, don't you?' Sameer tried to convince his friend.

'Of course I do,' Ravi was excited at the proposal.

'So, let's go,' they said together and ran towards the cars.

'Mum, Dad!' Sameer walked sheepishly to his parents, knowing his mother would make a scene, hugging him, kissing his face and embarrassing him in front of the whole school.

Ravi clicked a few pictures of his friend being hugged and fussed over like a baby.

'Don't,' Sameer protested, while being smothered by his mother.

'That is what best friends are for,' Ravi said with a fake evil laugh.

'You too, come here my dear!' Ravi, too, was pulled by Sameer's mother and shown affection in a similar way. It was now Sameer's turn to laugh at his friend.

'So, shall we leave now?' Sameer's dad asked the boys.

'Umm...Dad, Mum, can you guys do us a favour? It is kind of important...' Sameer told them about Asim, and his parents had no problem with taking the boys down the road to see their friend.

Finding Asim was a difficult job. The students, who were just getting off school, had thronged the ground, where the odd trio had once picked sweet mulberries and savoured them.

'Asim?' Sameer yelled at the top of his voice.

'Asim?' Ravi followed.

Some boys heard them and took them to Asim, who was in the science laboratory, finishing up some tasks and putting stuff away.

'You?' Asim asked. He was so surprised that he forgot to close his mouth and blink.

'Yeah, hi,' Ravi said, awkwardly.

'We came to say bye, actually,' Sameer said.

'Oh, so school is off?' Asim spoke from behind the huge desk, the same one where they had performed the experiment and filled a balloon with gas.

'I still have the balloon,' Sameer said.

'I told you,' Asim said with a grin.

'It deflated gradually, though,' Ravi added.

'And you still have it?' Asim asked Sameer.

'Yeah. I am a hoarder,' Sameer shrugged.

'We had a good time,' Asim said softly.

'So, all is good with you?' Ravi asked him with genuine concern.

'Yeah, I lost my job, of course...' His voice had a hint of disdain. Sameer lowered his head, feeling guilty.

'It has nothing to do with us, Asim,' Ravi said, fending for his friend.

'Oh I know. Just Rauf... He got carried away.'

'I guess,' Sameer said.

'Well, I'm all good, the school still pays me a stipend, basically a scholarship for deserving children, and I am paying my fees with that. So, no more dirty plates, only studies,' Asim said cheerfully, and the boys smiled.

'Friends?' Ravi said, extending his hand, and Asim shook it.

'Friends,' he said.

'Hey, you'll be back next year, won't you?'

'Absolutely,' Ravi replied.

They both felt happier as they walked towards the car where Sameer's parents were waiting for them. Ravi stayed back at the school until it was time for him to go back to his parents for the summer and prepare for another exciting new year with his friend Sameer, the school investigator.

EPILOGUE

Hiya Sameer!

What is up? What is down? How's life? Made any new friends? If so, why? Started your homework yet? I haven't.

Cuz...I'm going on a vacation! With my family, to Spain! You do remember, right? My dream place. Yay!! I am currently working on my Spanish. That stupid app of yours turned out to be actually pretty useful.

By the way, *como estas*? Don't think you'll get that one, now. Ha! Just reply with 'I am good'. Or you can just translate on Google. Or you can just pretend to know the language and lie and boast as you always do.

Anyway, I'm going to Granada and Barcelona, do the 'sightseeing bus thing' and visit the Casa Batlló Museum in Barcelona. Maybe next year, we'll even take the '3 countries tour in a day' trip to Mexico, Colombia and Chile. They're all Spanish-speaking countries, so I can definitely show off my wonderful, almost-perfect accent!

Hopefully, I'll see my favourite Spanish YouTubers

there too. I know you're making fun of me, but hey, a fan can dream.

Talking about passions, I got a new Xbox, and to say I am addicted, bro, would be an understatement. I can see Mum is mad at me, but I guess she'll just let me enjoy these few weeks of freedom. Think I broke the world record by playing it, dude, literally, 24x7.

I watch *La Casa de Papel* in my free time. I am obsessed with that too. But, for real, anyone who watches the first three minutes would be. Think I wanna rob the Royal Mint in Spain too. Only that I'll do it better than done in the drama series. Hey, you'll help me, won't you?

You tell me what is going on with you all? How's Pepper? How's the Chemistry laboratory? How are the sisters? Still teasing the freaking daylights out of you? Well, good on them, I am on their side! Tee hee.

I am really hopeful I get to be an exchange student next year as well. You remember the teacher from Delhi, Mr Verma? He already got his appointment letter, dude. So chances are, the same people are coming back at Kingston! Seriously, Kingston would so reek of boredom if it were not for the utterly butterly coolness of ahem ahem, Mr Handsome. You really need to learn a thing or two from me this year about style, kay?

Get your schedule in order before school. Mum has yelled at me to keep my butt out of trouble this year

(I know she is secretly proud of me) and I guess that is all. Got to go now!

Alrighty then. See ya, Nerd Face.

Ciao,
Ravi

༄

Hola Mr Handsome Ravi!

Estoy bien, for one, and you need to take my word. I did not Google it, you jackass. Remember, at the start of the year, I was the one who had become obsessed with Spanish. You're just a wannabe.

The sky's up, the ground is beneath my feet and I'm a loner, so no new friends. Homework is finished 'coz I'm not lazy. Mr Handsome needs to work on being a multitasker, or he will not have a friend anymore.

Pepper's good, the sisters are the same. I added some basic chemicals to my collection and I'm finally allowed to use some of those. Dad says I'm careful enough now. However, I did sneakily mix diluted versions of *those two chemicals* and and they reacted to produce a silver white liquid! Tried it on Pepper first, then myself. Figured that if Rauf could survive it, *my* dog could too, especially because it was a very diluted solution, comparatively. I only felt light-headed for a while. But very! So it's safe to say that everyone should learn from my experiences and not get into stupid situations!

Hey, I hope you don't meet your favourite YouTubers. I know how bad it hurts. I had a full list of celebrities to meet in London, but learnt in the news that they had all arrived a day after I had left or were very busy. You should *so* feel my pain. You deserve to, for doubting my Spanish skills. My vocab and enunciation are so much better than yours. I'll Skype you right after this to prove it. Be ready to be thoroughly embarrassed by your wrong claim.

In other news, I got a new guitar! Really obsessed. The bigger obsession though (*si!*), is with the same drama you named. *Money Heist* is what it's called in English. And I'm not a liar, so I watch the Spanish version, not the English one (*crèame!*) but with English subtitles. And I can almost hear you typing 'crèame' into Google Translate, 'coz you and I both know, you ain't that good at it!

Hey, I even started writing my own songs (but that's a secret) and don't even ask me to sing it to you, like you do every time, or I'll scream like a banshee right into your ear next time I see you. And that'll be all you'll get to hear of my voice.

Oh, and good luck to you for your Spain trip, really. I've roasted you enough on your Spanish. #sorrynotsorry.

And do return to Kingston!

Cheers,
Sameer

ACKNOWLEDGEMENTS

I want to thank my mother for being a constant source of encouragement throughout the writing process. This book wouldn't be possible without you! You are my biggest inspiration as a writer, but more significantly as a person and a woman—strong, resilient, as well as caring and kind. I cannot thank you enough.

My sister, Mumtaz, thank you for always reassuring me throughout my writer's block, and for listening to me rant about the multiple ideas I had for the book. Thanks to Zara, my little sister (super annoying), for pressing the backspace key and sabotaging my writing at every chance you could. Love you, though!

Thank you, Papa, for being there, always. I cannot thank you enough for your love!

To my best friend Tashfa, your undying obsession for books and reading was a huge motivation. I am grateful for your support and enthusiasm for the book throughout!

Thank you, my literary agent Suhail Mathur of The Book Bakers for taking a leap of faith and giving a headstart to my writing career, at 14!

Last but not least, I shall express my deepest gratitude to Rupa for providing me this platform for my debut novel. I will be forever grateful.

Made in the USA
Monee, IL
03 May 2026

49438406R00083